THE STAINED GLASS
WINDOWS OF
CANTERBURY CATHEDRAL

THE STAINED GLASS
WINDOWS OF
CANTERBURY CATHEDRAL

*A Guide for
Visitors and Students*

by

BERNARD RACKHAM

CANTERBURY

S · P · C · K

1957

First published in 1957
by S.P.C.K.
2 The Precincts
Canterbury
Made and printed in Great Britain by
William Clowes and Sons, Limited
London and Beccles
ALL RIGHTS RESERVED

TO
MARGARET BABINGTON
O.B.E.

CONTENTS

AUTHOR'S NOTE	7
INTRODUCTION	9
THE GENEALOGICAL WINDOWS	17
NORTH- AND SOUTH-EAST TRANSEPTS	21
APSE CLERESTORY	23
NORTH AND SOUTH CHOIR AISLES	23
NORTH CHOIR TRIFORIUM	34
SOUTH CHOIR TRIFORIUM	36
CRYPT	37
CORONA	39
NORTH-EAST TRANSEPT	46
SOUTH-EAST TRANSEPT	46
TRINITY CHAPEL AISLE	47
SOUTH-WEST TRANSEPT	69
WATER TOWER (EARLY GLASS)	69
EARLY REMNANTS, UNPLACED	70
NAVE	70
MUSIC ROOM	71
WEST WINDOW	71
WATER TOWER (LATE GLASS)	77
CHAPEL OF ST EDWARD THE CONFESSOR	79
SOUTH-WEST TRANSEPT	79
ST MICHAEL'S CHAPEL	84
LADY CHAPEL	85
NORTH-WEST TRANSEPT	86

5

WATER TOWER PASSAGE   94

LIBRARY CORRIDOR   95

LATE GOTHIC GLASS (UNPLACED)   95

GREAT CLOISTER   96

CHAPTER HOUSE   96

SUPPLEMENTARY NOTE   96

PLATES

1. Terah (now in South Window)   *facing p.* 16

2. The Miracle of Cana, North Choir
   Aisle, Window III   ,, 32

3. Crypt, East Window, upper part   ,, 36

4. King Josiah, from the "Tree of Jesse",
   Corona   ,, 44

5. Archbishop Becket appearing to
   Louis VII, Trinity Chapel,
   Window IV   ,, 48

6. The Story of Richard Sunieve,
   Trinity Chapel, Window VI   ,, 64

7. King, West Window   ,, 84

8. Queen Elizabeth Woodville, North
   Window   ,, 92

AUTHOR'S NOTE

THIS little book is the outcome of a good-humoured suggestion made to me by Mr Burgon Bickersteth: Could I provide, for the use of visitors studying the Canterbury windows on the spot, something more easy to carry than the great quarto to which reference is made below? I have written it in the hope that it may serve both to explain briefly the subjects depicted in the windows and, with these as illustrative material, as an introduction to the study of glass-painting. Those desiring more detailed information and a list of authorities are referred to my major work, *The Ancient Glass of Canterbury Cathedral*, published in 1949 for the Friends of Canterbury Cathedral by Messrs Lund Humphries, London, where also a full bibliography will be found.

I wish to record my gratefulness to Mr Bickersteth, as well as to several other friends for various assistance. My thanks are due first to Mr C. E. Sexton for valued help, especially for lending me colour films he has taken of the windows and for consenting to the use of some of them for illustrating this book; I have also to thank the Dean and Chapter and Miss Margaret Babington, Hon. Steward and Treasurer of the Friends of Canterbury Cathedral, for their concurrence, Mr William Urry, Keeper of Manuscripts in the Chapter Library, and Mr S. C. Caldwell for much information, my wife, for a critical reading of the proofs, and lastly Mr S. D. T. Spittle. My indebtedness to forerunners, the Reverend Canon J. M. C. Crum and the late Dr A. J. Mason, must not go unrecorded. Messrs Lund Humphries have generously lent for reproduction here the window diagrams from my earlier book. Finally, it is a pleasure to acknowledge the courteous and willing co-operation I have received from the publishers, the Society for Promoting Christian Knowledge.   BERNARD RACKHAM

INTRODUCTION

THOUGH traceable to Byzantine origins, stained glass is essentially an art of Western Europe; its earliest surviving examples show it already developed beyond the rudimentary stage. Its technique was established at the time when the system of vaulted construction had taken shape as the characteristic feature of the Romanesque architecture of France and adjacent lands; from this it became an integral element in the Gothic system of construction which grew out of the Romanesque.

It may fairly be said that in the planning of any cathedral or major church of the 12th or following centuries until the end of the Middle Ages stained glass was counted on as an essential part of the fabric. Improvements in the roofing system made larger windows feasible; by filling these with glass-paintings it was possible, in appearance, to avoid the resultant discontinuity in the enclosing walls which was abhorrent to the builders in climates where shelter from the elements was needed; a church had to be essentially a space marked off, physically as well as metaphorically, from the secular world outside.

In not many places was this ideal realized to the full; in fewer still has this realization survived intact or unrestored till the present day. It can be seen at its best only in France, at Chartres, supremely, and in such buildings as Bourges Cathedral, or the Sainte Chapelle in Paris. In England it is to be found perhaps most completely at York Minster, or in certain college chapels at Oxford and Cambridge, notably King's; but for its earliest exemplification it can nowhere be better studied, or more logically, than at Canterbury Cathedral, in spite of the sad mutilation the windows there have suffered with the passage of time. The windows of Canterbury stand out among the relics of medieval art not only by reason of their beauty and high quality as design but also as illustrations of Christian iconography.

Stained-glass windows came to have not only a practical and a decorative function; they were also enlisted as a means of conveying pictorially the doctrines of Christianity. They served the same purpose as the paintings in fresco on the broad wall-surfaces of Italian churches; they gave space for a series of illustrations either of Bible history and the symbolical teaching based upon it, or of the works and martyrdom of the saint to whom the church was dedicated. Like fresco-painting, they were closely related to the pictures in illuminated manuscripts of the period on which probably they were sometimes based and for which on occasion they may have provided suggestions.[1] Perhaps no other cathedral, even in France, offers a better example of the consistent carrying-out of a didactic or illustrative scheme than Canterbury; King's College Chapel and Fairford Church provide parallels more perfectly conserved, but these are both of a late period when the art of glass-painting was on the edge of eclipse.

For the better understanding of what follows by those unfamiliar with the subject, a summary may be given in the briefest terms of the technique of the art. It needs to be stressed that few coloured windows are of stained glass alone, entirely without brushwork. The art is in effect a kind of painting, decorative or pictorial, composed of pieces of coloured glass having details of the design painted on them in black enamel pigment with a brush; sometimes these details are executed "in reserve", by scratching with the stick of the brush or a needle point through a solid layer of black or grey pigment. This very effective technique is illustrated by the superb inscriptions in Lombardic lettering on many of the earliest windows in the Cathedral. The painted glass, which could be produced in larger pieces or panes as the manufacture of glass improved, is held together by flexible strips of lead which could be made to outline and give accent to the constituent elements of the pattern or picture; for their support, the leaded panels or

[1] Compare p. 19 below.

medallions, of which any but quite small windows were made up, needed an iron framework or "armature". As is superbly shown at Canterbury, these armatures themselves could play an important part not only structurally but also in the effectiveness of the windows as design. With the development of stone mullions and tracery in the 13th century and later, the window areas came to be divided into smaller units; the stone-work itself largely provided the needful framework, so that the iron supports could be restricted to horizontal "saddle-bars" at convenient levels.

Among other developments of technique those of the greatest importance relate to the painting of the glass. Late in the 13th century, in France, a stain was invented made of chloride of silver, which on being fired on the surface of the glass imparted a yellow or golden colour (when applied to blue glass it produced green); this was of great value in enabling, for instance, a crown and a face, or sky and a tree, to be rendered by means of a single piece of glass where two, separated by a lead, had been necessary before. Other "enamel" pigments—first red, then blue and purple—were invented towards the end of the Middle Ages, so that at last in the 17th century, it became possible and customary to make up a window of rectangular panes of plain white glass, these enamel colours together with the silver-yellow stain being employed to provide the desired colouring.

Another helpful innovation arose from the peculiar charac-ter of "ruby" glass. The colouring medium, copper, acts so powerfully that light barely penetrates a glass sheet of any thickness stained with it; ruby was therefore made by "flash-ing". This was done in the process of blowing the glass: a lump of plain white glass was dipped into molten glass stained red with copper and then blown to form a white bulb with a thin ruby film on the outside; the pane made from this bulb by the usual process showed a ruby "flash" on one of its surfaces. It was found that this ruby film could be ground away to reveal the white, giving a white pattern on a red ground; the exposed white could be stained with silver-yellow to make a pattern in yellow and red. From the 14th century onwards, this process was found a great convenience—especially in heraldry, when small charges had to be rendered.

Apart from scanty remnants at York and a small window at Brabourne, Kent, Canterbury possesses the oldest stained glass in England, dating before the end of the 12th century. Nothing remains of the painted windows one may assume to have existed in the church built by Archbishop Lanfranc and enlarged by priors Ernulph and Conrad. The earliest surviving windows belong to those parts of the cathedral erected after the fire of 1174 by William of Sens and his successor, the reconstructed Choir and Transepts, and the eastward extension carried out as a sequel to this rebuilding, to accommodate the shrine of St Thomas Becket. These are the windows of the Clerestory, all of which retain their original iron armatures; less than half their original glazing survives, and that mostly removed to other parts of the building, as will be explained on a later page. By means of a series of isolated figures these windows illustrated a single theme, the descent of Christ from Adam, interrupted only by the three middle windows of the Apse depicting the most important incidents from his Life and Passion. The westernmost may be dated about 1178 or a little before, and with them probably the two rose-windows of the Eastern Transepts, with their subjects symbolizing the Old and New Dispensations; those of the Trinity Chapel, further east, show a perceptible change of style and are by a few years more recent. Next in order of date may be placed the "Theological" windows of the Choir Aisles, about 1200, displaying Gospel scenes with their Old Testament forerunners, together with the east window of the Crypt, the former Lady Chapel, beneath the Corona. A development in the style of foliage suggests a date at the beginning of the 13th century for the east window of the Corona itself (in which the teaching of the "Theological" windows is summarized in a single composition) and probably those which formerly flanked it. The aisle triforium windows of the Choir, on one side scriptural, on the other devoted to SS. Dunstan and Alphege, are of about the same date, as also a (restored) window in the Water Tower.

The ambulatory windows of the Trinity Chapel are of the

second or third decade of the 13th century; they formed, until many of them were destroyed, a continuous series glorifying the sainted archbishop whose shrine they surrounded.

More than half a century separates these windows from the great West window which, in its unaltered state, splendidly displayed the art, in the altered manner prevalent at the end of the 14th century and a few decades later; fragments from the same period are to be found in some North Aisle windows of the Nave. Compared with the arresting colour of the earlier, 13th century glass, with its dominant deep blue and ruby, windows of this second phase of Gothic are marked by a more subtle appeal to the eye; they show a liking for greens of various tones, mauve, brown, and a more sombre crimson, combined with the golden shades obtainable by means of the silver-yellow stain. The shields of the West window tracery and those of the somewhat later great South-West Transept window of the time of Archbishop Chichele prove the magnificence by this time attained in heraldic design.

English glass-painting of the 15th century, up to the period when with the approach of the Renaissance there was a return to lavish and brilliant colour, is in general marked by a luminous clarity owing to the large proportion of white glass adopted, the cool tones of silver-yellow, and the restraint imposed on the use of other colours, with a tendency to restrict them to blue and ruby. All this was in conformity with a disposition to profit by the vast windows now available through the development of vaulting and Perpendicular tracery, for the admission of a flood of light, perhaps deliberately designed to give effect to the elaborate sculptures of altars, tombs, and chantries with which churches were commonly adorned. This period is perhaps less adequately represented at Canterbury than elsewhere, as for instance in the Choir at York, at Great Malvern, or at Ludlow; but enough remains in the shape of small figure-panels such as those in the Chapel of St Edward the Confessor and the Water Tower, many of them now no longer in their original situations. The heraldry, the small medallions with armorial badges, and the decorative "*grisaille*" (glass with painting in black only, usually picked out with silver-yellow) of this period are admirably exemplified in the Bourchier windows of the Lady Chapel and those of St Michael's Chapel. Late Gothic glass-painting justified itself in a final burst of achievement by the productions of the royal workshop at Westminster; to this workshop may be attributed the portraits and shields of the great window in the North-West Transept, presumed to have been given by Edward IV, magnificent still, though now sadly defective and rearranged. Inserted in this are a radiant example of Tudor heraldic design and, interestingly contrasted with it, a small foreign panel in which Renaissance motives are already in evidence. Although Canterbury has no major work in the enamel-painting technique which was all-pervading after the Reformation, the process and its drawbacks can be sufficiently appreciated from a small Elizabethan shield and two panels with arms relating to Archbishop Abbot (1611–33).

For the convenience of those who desire to study systematically the development of the art of glass-painting as illustrated at Canterbury Cathedral the subjoined sequence is recommended in examining the windows; by whichever door the Cathedral is entered, the visitor should go first into the Choir.

Choir. Clerestory windows (pp. 18, 19).

Nave. Early panels in West window (pp. 19, 20).

South-West Transept. Early panels in South Window (pp. 20, 21).

St Andrew's Chapel. Early panel (p. 21).

East Transepts. Rose windows (p. 21).

Trinity Chapel. Apse Clerestory windows (p. 23).

North Choir Aisle. Aisle windows and South Triforium windows (pp. 23, 34, 36).

South Choir Aisle. North Triforium windows (p. 34).

Crypt (p. 37).

Corona (p. 39).

North-East Transept. St Martin's Chapel (p. 46).

Trinity Chapel. Aisle windows (p. 47).

Water Tower. Early glass (p. 69).

Nave. Aisle windows (p. 70).

Nave. West window (p. 71).
Water Tower. Late glass (p. 77).
St Edward's Chapel (p. 79).
South-West Transept.[1] Later glass (p. 79).
St Michael's Chapel (p. 84).
Lady Chapel (p. 85).
North-West Transept[1] (p. 86).
Water Tower Passage and *Library Corridor* (pp. 94, 95).

The 19th-century and later windows are for convenience named, with their artists, in the places where they occur among those of earlier periods; the most important are in the Nave, the Western and Eastern Transepts, St Michael's Chapel, St Andrew's Chapel, the Chapter House, and the Great Cloister.

[1] The great South and North windows can be seen best from the steps under the Bell Harry Tower.

PLATE I. TERAH (NOW IN SOUTH WINDOW).
LATE 12TH CENTURY.

facing p. 16

THE GENEALOGICAL WINDOWS

CLERESTORY OF CHOIR, EASTERN
TRANSEPTS, AND TRINITY CHAPEL

THE clerestory windows of the eastern half of the cathedral were designed to illustrate by a series of figures, two in each window, the descent of Christ from Adam, as recorded in Luke 3; eight additional figures were included, from Matthew 1, in order to make up the requisite number of eighty-four. The first window, at the west end of the Choir, on the north, showed the Almighty creating Adam in its upper half and Adam delving below; the last, facing it, brought the series to an end with the Virgin Mary and our Lord. All the surviving figures except Adam are seated on a throne or chair. The sequence was interrupted by five windows in the Apse, of which three, each comprising three panels, were devoted to the most important incidents in the Life and Passion of Christ from the Nativity to the Ascension (see p. 36); flanking these one on each side, were two windows by George Austin, relating to Moses and St John the Baptist as the first and last of the Prophets (the subjects of their original glass are not recorded).

There is a perceptible difference in treatment and disposition between the windows in the western part of the series and all, save the first two on each side, in the Trinity Chapel; of the former, all but those in the first six windows were originally set under shrine-like arched canopies, and may be assumed to date from about 1178; the remainder, in the Trinity Chapel, though they must have been part of the intended scheme from the first, were evidently executed later, about the beginning of the 13th century, and from cartoons by a different designer; the figures are enclosed in panels of various outlines.

All the clerestory windows retain their original iron armatures; of the figure-panels, only nine now remain in the clerestory, and of these only three (Nos. 15, 23 and 61) are in their original places, the rest having been shifted from window to window. Fourteen of the windows still show their ancient borders, which are notable for their powerful foliage designs and are entirely Romanesque in feeling. The remaining figures that survive are now distributed in the West window of the Nave and the South window of the South-West Transept (to which they were removed in 1792) and in a window of St Andrew's Chapel. They are described below as in their present several locations and, in each place, in their original sequence in the series (indicated by the numerals in brackets following their names). With the exception of the eight figures mentioned above and fourteen borders the windows were filled with modern glass by George Austin in 1861–2, copying or imitating the ancient glass. Austin's work was partly destroyed during the air attack of 1942 and has now been restored by Mr Caldwell; he took this opportunity of inserting in the upper half of the first window the original 12th-century face of Adam, which he had come across, and two other heads, reproduced in the author's *Ancient Glass of Canterbury Cathedral*, pl. 50a, 64a.

BORDERS

The original borders remain in the following windows (numbered from left to right):

> *Choir*, north side—Windows 1, 3, 5.
> *North-East Transept*, west side—Window 1.
> *North-East Transept*, east side—Windows 3, 4.
> *Trinity Chapel*, north side—Windows 1, 4, 5, 7; in No. 5 the groundwork is also ancient, slightly restored.
> *Trinity Chapel*, south side—Windows 6, 7, 9.
> *South-East Transept*, east side—Windows 1, 2.

FIGURES NOW IN CLERESTORY

North-East Transept, west side, Window 3:

> *Heber* (15). Inscr. (defective): ..BER. The lower half restored by S. C. Caldwell, 1955.

North-East Transept, east side, Window 4:

> *Shem* (12), holding a scroll. Inscr.: SEM.
> *Isaac* (23). Throne painted to imitate porphyry. Inscr. (defective): I...C. This figure is in its original position.

South-East Transept, east side, Window 1:

> *Neri* (61). Inscr.: NERI (in original position).
> *Rhesa* (64), holding a scroll. Inscr.: RESA. (Wrongly identified by Westlake as Esaias.)

South-East Transept, east side, Window 2:

> *Judah* (25), holding a scroll. Inscr.: IVDA.
> *Phares* (26), with scroll. Inscr.: PHARES.

South-East Transept, east side, Window 3:

> Unidentified, perhaps *Matthat* (52) or *Maath* (70). Inscr. (defective): M...AT. Unidentified.

NAVE (WEST WINDOW)

The references preceding the names are to the diagram of the window (p. 72).

L.4   *Adam* (2), girt with a fleece and delving with a mattock, Inscr.: ADAM. The figure may be compared with that closely similar but on a miniature scale at the beginning of the Bible of Robert of Battle (de Bello), Abbot of St Augustine's (1224–53), which was doubtless copied from it or from an original common to both; in later MSS. Adam commonly wears a shirt.

L.1   *Esrom* (27), with scroll. Inscr.: ESROM.

L.7   *Aram* (28), with scroll. Inscr.: ARAN(*sic*).

L.6   *Aminadab* (29), with scroll. Inscr. (defective): ...H(?) A...AD.

L.2   *Naasson* (30). Inscr.: NAASON.

I.2   *Obed* (33), with scroll. Inscr.: OBETH.

I.6   *Jesse* (34), with scroll. Inscr.: IESSE.

I.3   *Rehoboam* (37), with scroll. Inscr.: ROBOAS.

I.5   *Abia* (38), with scroll. Inscr.: ABIAS.

I.1   Perhaps *Jechonias* (41), holding a book and a bowl full of coins. Inscr. illegible.

I.7   Perhaps *Salathiel* (42). Inscr. (defective): SI...C.

L.5   *Joseph* (67). Inscr. (partly restored): *IOSE*PH.[1]

L.3   *Semei* (68), holding a book or scroll (exceptional in being beardless). Inscr. (incorrectly restored): SE*TH*.

SOUTH-WEST TRANSEPT
(SOUTH WINDOW)

The references preceding the names are to the diagram of the window (p. 80).

Q.4   *Jared* (7). Inscr.: *IA*RETH.

Q.8   *Enoch* (8). He looks up towards the hand of God extended from a cloud and seizing his wrist for his "translation" to Heaven. Inscr.: ENOCH.

Q.5   *Methuselah* (9). Inscr.: MATVSALE.

Q.1   *Lamech* (10), on throne with high arcaded back. Inscr. (restored): LAM*E*CH.

Q.2   *Noah* (11). Inscr.: NOE.

Q.6   *Phalec* (17), with scroll. Inscr.: PHALECH.

Q.7   *Ragau* (18), with scroll. Inscr.: RAGAV.

Q.3   *Terah* (21), with scroll. Inscr.: THARE.   (Pl. 1)

M.1   *Abraham* (22). Inscr.: ABRAM (the usual form of M may be noted).

H.4   *David* (35), supporting a scroll inscribed: DAVID.

H.5   *Nathan* (36), holding a sceptre topped with a dove. Inscr.: NATHAN.

M.5   *Hezekiah* (39). He holds the Dial of Ahaz, in allusion to the shadow turning backward on the sundial (2 Kings 20. 8–11). Inscr.: EZECHIAS.

M.6   *Josiah* (40), holding the Book of the Law (in the form of a long scroll inscribed with mock Hebrew characters), in allusion to its re-discovery (2 Kings 22. 8—23. 2). Inscr.: IOSIAS.

[1] Here and throughout this *Guide* italicized capitals in inscriptions are either interpolations or modern restorations. Deficiencies which can be made good without question are inserted in roman capitals between square brackets []; small italics are used for explanatory insertions.

H.6	Unidentified, possibly *Jonan* (47). In "Phrygian" cap. Inscr. (defective) : ACLC(?).
H.3	Unidentified, with sceptre, possibly *Joseph* (48). Inscr. (disordered, and perhaps belonging to another figure) : IOSEP.
H.7	*Jose* (55), with scroll. Inscr. (mutilated) : *L*ESV.
H.2	*Er* (56). Inscr. : HER.
M.8	*Zorobabel* (63). Inscr. : ZOROBABEL.
H.1	*Joanna* (63). Inscr. : JOHANNA.
H.8	*Juda* (66), with scroll. Inscr. : IVDE.
M.2	Unidentified, perhaps *Salmon* (31).
M.7	Unidentified, perhaps *Boaz*. Head modern.

FIGURE NOW IN ST ANDREW'S CHAPEL, WEST SIDE

Cosam (58), beardless, with scroll. Inscr. (defective) : CO . . . (?). Restored and set in its present place in 1928.

FRAGMENT, UNPLACED

The bearded head of an unidentified figure from one of the earlier windows of the series.

NORTH- AND SOUTH-EAST TRANSEPTS

ROSE WINDOWS

THE north rose may be dated about 1178; it retains its original armature. It has for its subject the Old Dispensation, "the Law and the Prophets", represented by Moses and the Synagogue surrounded by the Cardinal Virtues and the four Major Prophets, with foliated ornament in the interspaces. The outer part of the window was supplied early in the present century with figures of the eight Minor Prophets, designed by

S. C. Caldwell under the direction of Canon A. J. Mason, set among foliated ornament partly made up of original 12th-century glass.

1, 2   *Moses and the Synagogue.* Moses holds the tables of stone delivered on Sinai (in the form of a jewelled book) ; the Synagogue is represented as a woman with the Tables of the Law. The faces of both figures were restored by George Austin, Junior; that of the Synagogue was probably originally blindfolded, as commonly in medieval art (e.g., the statues at Strasburg and Rochester). Inscr. (restored): MOY*SES, SINA*GOG.

3   *Prudence*, with dragon-like serpent in one hand and two doves in the other. Inscr.: PRVDEN.

4   *Justice*, with scales and a scroll inscribed: IVSTICIA; below the scales a bag (?) of unexplained significance.

5   *Temperance*, with torch in one hand and a bowl of water in the other. Inscr.: TEMPANTIA.

6   *Fortitude*, with sword and a green twisted cord. Inscr.: FORTITVDO.

7   *Isaiah*. Inscr.: YSAIAS.

8   *Jeremiah*. Inscr.: IEREMIA P(*ropheta*).

9   *Ezekiel*. Inscr: EZECHIEL.

10   *Daniel*. Inscr.: DANIEL.

The south rose contains much of its original background of foliage. The figures were supplied in 1850 by George Austin, Junior, doubtless correctly, to illustrate the New Dispensation: Christ and the Church in the centre, surrounded by the Symbols of the Evangelists, the Christian Virtues (Faith, Hope, Charity, and Humility) and eight of the Apostles.

TRIFORIUM

The innermost windows on the east side of the North-East and South-East Transepts contain figures in 12th-century style by Samuel Caldwell, senior, about 1895–1900, set in 12th-century borders and groundwork: (N.E.) *Enud* (*sic*), *Shamgar, Barak*, and *Gideon* ; (S.E.) *SS. Peter, Stephen, Paul, Barnabas*.

APSE CLERESTORY

THE five windows of the apse made a break in the "Genealogical" series (compare p. 17). They were filled in 1861–2 with modern compositions in medallions, by George Austin, Junior, as follows: (1) *The Giving of the Law; Moses Striking the Rock*. (2) *The Adoration of the Magi; The Agony in the Garden; The Transfiguration*. (3) *The Nativity; The Crucifixion; The Ascension*. (4) *The Flight into Egypt; The Flagellation; The Resurrection*. (5) *The Beheading of St John the Baptist; The Baptism*. These were destroyed by the bombardment of 1942. The middle window (3) was filled by S. C. Caldwell in 1947, within the original border, with a trellis-pattern largely of 13th-century glass surrounding a medallion of the *Crucifixion* composed by himself; in this, only portions of the figure of Christ are ancient.

NORTH AND SOUTH
CHOIR AISLES

THE windows of the Choir Aisles and those of the two Eastern Transepts at the lowest level originally formed a series of twelve, sometimes known as the "Theological Windows"; they illustrate "Types" and "Antitypes", that is, New Testament subjects (including the Parables) and the incidents foreshadowing them, as types, in the Old Testament. The scheme was codified in the 13th century in the *Biblia Pauperum* ("Poor Man's Bible").

The windows date from about the beginning of the 13th century; a 14th-century manuscript in the Chapter Library gives a catalogue of their subjects and copies of their inscriptions. The first window of the series was blocked when stairs to the organ-loft formerly above the adjacent choir-stalls were constructed. The remnants of the residue are now gathered together in two windows of the North Choir Aisle, in each of which are a few panels that belonged there from the beginning; both are noticeable for their fine borders, still Romanesque in character. The inscriptions are in some cases in Leonine hexameter verse. In the descriptions given below the Antitypes are cited before the Types which accompany them, one on each side—so far as they survive in their original relationship.

WINDOW II

The upper panels, numbered 1 to 14, are in their original positions; the lower, Nos. 15–21, are insertions brought from Window VI.

1–3 (2) *The Ride of the Magi.* They point towards the Star among clouds above; the leader is already entering Jerusalem. (1) *Balaam,* stretching his hands towards the Star in the middle panel. Inscr.: BALAAM and ORIETVR STELLA EX IACOB ET CONSVRGET VIRGA DE ISRAEL ("There shall come a star out of Jacob, and a sceptre shall rise out of Israel"). (3) *Isaiah and Jerusalem.* The prophet stands at the gate of (presumably) Jerusalem, pointing towards the star. Inscr.: YSA and AMBVLABVNT GENTES IN LVMINE TVO ET REGES IN SPLENDORE ORT' *BENIAMs* ("The Gentiles shall come to thy light, and kings to the brightness of thy rising"). The last word, replacing one that has been lost, probably belonged to a lost circle at the foot of the window, with the Slaughter of the Tribe of Benjamin (Judges 20).

4–6 (5) *Herod and the Magi.* He listens to their narrative; a priest or scribe stands behind, perhaps telling where Christ should be born. Inscr.: TRES MAGI, HERODES. (4) *The Exodus.* Pharaoh, with crown and sceptre, at the door of his house, dismissing Moses; on the left, Moses, rod in hand, pointing towards the Red Sea and leading a group of Israelites; above is the Pillar of Fire as a flaming column. Inscr.: PHARAO REX EGIPTI; ISRL SEQVENS COLVMPNAM ("Israel

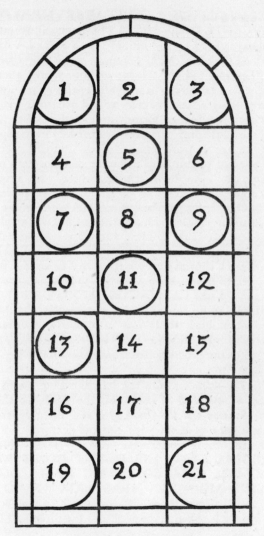

NORTH CHOIR AISLE II

following the pillar"); EXIT AB ERVMP*NA POP*LVS DVCENTE CO*LVMP*NA ("The people go out of the wilderness led by the pillar"), and STELLA MAGOS DVXIT: LVX XPC (*Christus*) VTRISQ RELVXIT ("The star led the Magi; to both Christ shone as a light"). The border at the sides of this panel, somewhat resembling a series of crowns and occurring frequently, in slightly modified forms, through the earlier windows of the Cathedral, is derived ultimately from repetitions of the Arabic word *Allah* ("God"), in Cufic script[1]; it is often to be found as a motive of decoration in Saracenic art, notably in textiles, which were brought to Europe and served as copies to Christian designers.

(6) *Christ leading the heathen out of idolatry.* On the right is a heathen temple, with a horned idol above an altar. On the left, our Lord, holding a scroll to represent the Gospel, leads a group of men, some of whom look back, towards a church with a cross above an altar and a font; a winged devil above attempts to dissuade the people. Inscr.: STELLA MAGOS DVXIT; ET EOS AB HERODE REDVXIT ("A star led the Wise Men and led them back to Herod"), and SIC SATHANAM GENTES FVGIVNT TE XPE (*Christe*) SEQVENTES ("Thus the Gentiles flee from Satan, following thee, O Christ").

7–9   (8) *The Adoration.* On the left, the Magi, with caskets and a bowl full of coins, on the right the shepherd. (7) *Solomon and the Queen of Sheba.* Behind her, attendants (one of them with negroid features) with three camels bring offerings. Inscr.: REX SALOM: REGINA SABA; HIS DONAT DONIS REGINA DOMVM SALOMONIS. SIC REGES DOMINO DANT M[VN]ERA TRES TRIA TRINO ("The Queen bestows these gifts on the house of Solomon. Thus the kings give three gifts to the three-fold Lord").

[1] Not *alafia* ("blessing") as hitherto supposed by the author (see *The Archaeological Journal* CXI, 1951, S. D. T. Spittle, "Cufic lettering in Christian Art", p. 148).

(9) *Joseph and his Brethren.* Joseph enthroned between his brethren and Egyptians; some carry bowls with coins. Inscr.: IOSEPH, F R̃S (*fratres*) IOSEPH + EGIPTII, AD TE LONGINQVOS IOSEPH ATTRAHIS ATQ' PROPINQVOS: SIC DE*VCI* (for *Deus*) INCVNIS IVDEOS GENTIBVS VNIS ("Thou, Joseph, drawest to thyself men from far and near: thus, O God, thou dost unite Jews and Gentiles at the cradle [of Christ]").

10–12 (11) *The Dream of the Magi.* The Three Kings asleep in bed, crowned; above, an angel with a scroll inscribed: NE R(*e*)DEATIS AD HERODEM ("Return not to Herod"). (10) *Lot's Escape from Sodom.* On the left, two angels lead him with his daughters away from the burning city towards which his wife (already turned into a pillar of salt, as shown by the white glass employed), standing in the middle, looks back. Inscr.: VT LOTH SAL[V]ETVR NE RESPICIAT PROHIBETVR, SIC VITANT REVEHI PER HERODIS REGNA SABEI ("Lot is forbidden to look back so that he may be saved; so the Sabaeans avoid riding back through the realms of Herod"). (12) *Jeroboam's Sacrifice* (1 Kings 13. 9). The "man of God", entitled PPH'A (*Propheta*), with a flock of sheep, approaches King Jeroboam who, with attendants, is about to slaughter a lamb on an altar; beside it, a vessel for wine or the blood. Inscr.: NE REDEAS VIA Q(*u*)A VENISTI ("Return not by the way by which thou camest") on a scroll held by a hand emerging from a cloud; REX IEROBOAM; VT MVTETVR REDEVNDO PPH'A MONETVR SIC TRES EGERVNT QVI XPO DONA TVLER-VNT ("The prophet is warned that his road should be changed as he returns; thus did the three act who brought gifts to Christ").

13–14 (14) *The Presentation in the Temple* (Candlemas). The Virgin holds the infant Christ above the altar towards the outstretched hands of Simeon, behind whom is an attendant holding a long white candle with ruby flame;

27

Joseph follows the Virgin, with a candle and two doves in a basket. (13) *Eli receiving Samuel.* The priest (HELI SACERDOS) at an altar stretches his hands towards Samuel, who is followed by his parents Elkanah and Hannah and a woman with an amphora of wine, also three bullocks for sacrifice; on the altar, the Ark containing Aaron's rod, the Tables of the Law, and a pot of manna; below, three baskets with corn. It may be noted that the scene conforms with the Vulgate, not with the Authorized Version. Inscr.: SIGNIFICAT DOMINVM SAMVEL PVER AMPHORA VINVM ..*A..RE*: [NATV]RA GEMINVM TRIPLEX OBLATIO TRINVM ("The child Samuel signifies the Lord, the amphora the wine; the threefold offering the triune form of that which is by nature twofold"). The companion, *Abraham and Melchisedech*, lost.

Seven panels from Window VI, described in their original order

15, 17 (15) *The Parable of the Sower* (first scene). Some of the seed falls on a road where it is devoured by birds of various colours, other lies on "stony ground" (rocks and yellow soil). (17) *Christ abandoned by the Pharisees* (John 6. 66). Inscr.: NISI MANDVCAVERITIS CARNEM F(*ilii*) *HEBES NEVIVS* (on the scroll held by our Lord, "Except ye eat the flesh of the Son of Man"); SEMEN RORE CARENS EXPERS RADICIS ET ARENS HI SVNT QVI CREDVNT. TENTANTVR SICQ; RECEDVNT ("Seed lacking dew, having no root and parched, these are they who believe, are tempted, and thus fall back").

19–21 (20) *The Parable of the Sower* (second scene). In the foreground, thorn-bushes; the bare soil of the good ground behind with seed scattered over it. The inscription: ..IDIATOR, inserted from elsewhere. (19) *The deceitfulness of Riches*, personified by IVLIANVS and MAVRICIVS—the Emperors Julian the Apostate and Maurice (the opponent of St Gregory), with attendants; a bowl heaped with coins between them, their fur-lined mantles thrown over a rail above. Inscr. (defective and disordered): DELICIOSI NIL FRVCTVS REFERVNT QVON*TNE* [displacing IAM] TERRESTRIA QVERVNT...NOSI (The inscription originally began: *Isti spinosi locupletes deliciosi*, "These thorny ones are the rich and luxurious; they bear nought of fruit since they seek earthly things"). (21) *The good ground*, personified by Job, Daniel, and Noah, the three righteous men of Ezek. 14. 14. They hold scrolls with their names: DANIEL, IOB, NOE: three angels descend from a cloud to set three-pointed crowns on their heads. Noah rests one foot on a rainbow. Inscr. (disordered): VERBA PATRIS SEVIT DEV...ONA CTVS SIBI CREVIT: IN TELLVRE BON SVA (*Verba Patris sevit deus hijs fructus sibi crevit. In tellure bona triplex sua cuique corona*, "God sowed the words of the Father; to these fruit was brought forth. In the good ground to each was given a triple crown"). The medallion has been cut and completed by part of another from the same window, with the *Parable of the Draw-net*, inscr.: REPROBANTVR: PARS EST A DO[MINO]... ("These who are cast to the left are they that are rejected; this part, cursed by the Lord, is destined to be burnt in the furnace").

16, 18 These panels originally flanked, as their antitype, the *Parable of the Leaven* or *Three Measures of Meal*. (16) *The Church and the three sons of Noah*, symbolical of it. The Church, with title *ECCLE*SIA, as a woman holding a scroll with a mock inscription; beside her, SEM, CH*EV* (Ham), and IAPHET supporting the world (MVNDVS), which is divided between them into three portions, variously coloured, and encircled by an inscription: PARTE NOE NATI MICHI QVISQ; SVA DOMINATI ("Noah's sons ruling for me, each in his own part"). Inscr. (above): VNA FIDES NATIS EX HIS TRIBVS ET [for *est*] DEITITATIS ("From these three sons one faith in the Godhead").

The inscription below is made up of fragments from other windows in the series: VERIT SVM P RO S EO DE ABEL DE SH BORAT (Elijah's flight from Jezebel and Ahab—*insidias Jezabel declinat Helyas*—as type of the Flight into Egypt—*sic Deus Herodem terrore remotus eodem*), and Peter fishing—*mundi cura laborat*—while John prays. (18) *The three blameless states of life*, Virginity, Continence, and Marriage, typified by men holding scrolls with inscriptions (VIRGO, CONTINENS, CONIVGATVS) filled out with mock characters, apparently Hebrew, Arabic, and Latin. Inscr.: above and below: [FERMENTATA S]ATA TRIA TRES FRVCTVS OPERATA SVNT VXO-RATIS ET VIRGINIBVS VIDVATIS ("Three seeds when leavened produce three fruits, for the espoused, the virgin, and the widowed").

WINDOW III

Of the original pictorial panels only one medallion (No. 1) and three half-medallions (Nos. 2, 3, 8) now remain; the rest are interpolations from other windows of the series, here described in their original sequence. The fine original vine-pattern border, with grapes, should be noticed, and the blue grounds of the medallions, both pictorial and with foliage, set off by the ruby ground of the interspaces, with their leafy stems.

1–3 (1) *Christ among the Doctors*. He sits with a scroll in his hand amidst eight bearded men, one of whom holds an open book. Inscr.: IHC DVODENNIS IN MEDIO DOCTORVM ("The twelve-year-old Jesus in the midst of the doctors"). (2) *Moses and Jethro*. The prophet (MOYSES) receiving advice from the Gentile (IETHRO) (Ex. 18. 13–26) is a type of the humility of Christ. Inscr.: HIC HOMINES AVDIT DS (*Deus*). HINC VIR SANCTVS OBAVDIT GENTILIS VERBIS. HVMILES SVNT FORMA SVPERVIS. ("Here God listens to men. Hence the holy man pays heed to the words of the Gentile. The humble are the

NORTH CHOIR AISLE III

pattern for the proud.") (3) *Daniel among the Elders.*
Daniel judging the guilty Elders (Susanna 50–60) as a
type of the wisdom of the boy Christ. Inscr.: DANIEL
and MIRANTVR PVERI SENIORES VOCE
DOCERI SIC RESPONSA [*Dei sen*]SVMQVE
STVPENT PHARISEI ("The Elders marvel at being
taught by the utterances of a boy; thus the Pharisees
are amazed at the answers of God").

8   *Noah in the Ark* (type of the Baptism). He is opening
the window to let in the dove returning with the olive-
branch. Inscr.: NOE IN ARCHA and FLVXV
CVNCTA VAGO SVBMERGENS PRIMA
VORAGO OMNIA PVRGAVIT BAPTISMAQVE
SIGNIFICAVIT ("The first devouring flood, sub-
merging everything with its pervading flow, purified
all things and signified baptism").

Six panels from Window IV

10   *The calling of Nathanael.* Two scenes combined: to right,
NATHANAEL under the fig tree (FICVS), in medita-
tion, Philip (PHILIPP') points to where Jesus stands.
In the middle, Nathanael (with name) repeated, with
a scroll inscribed: VNDE ME NOS*TI* ("Whence
knowest thou me?"); our Lord meets him, with a
scroll inscribed: CV*M* EES (*esses*) S[*ub ficu*] VIDI [*te*]
("When thou wast beneath the fig tree I saw thee").
Two disciples (PETRVS and ANDREAS) stand by.

4   *The Miracle of Cana.* Our Lord seated to right, with his
Mother between him and a disciple; to the left, the
bride and bridegroom, and the mitred governor of the
feast, to whom a servant offers a bowl of wine; another
receiving instructions from Christ is filling six waterpots.
Among the viands a symbolical fish in a bowl. The diaper
on the table-cloth is painted on the outside of the glass
(Pl. 2).

5   *The Six Ages of the World*, referring to the six waterpots
in No. 4; represented by ADAM (with hoe), NOE
(with the Ark), ABRAH(*am*) (with fire in a bowl and

32

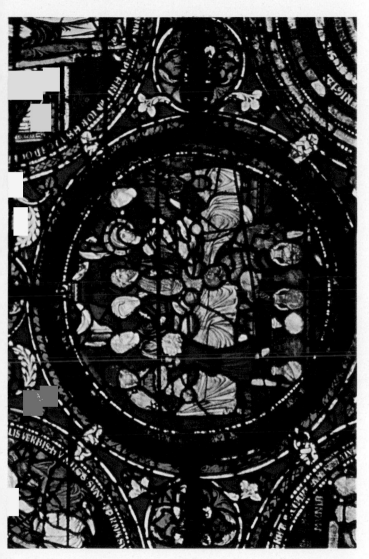

PLATE 2. THE MIRACLE OF CANA. EARLY 13TH CENTURY. NORTH CHOIR AISLE, WINDOW III. P. 32.

sword), DAVID (crowned, with harp), IECHONIAS (with crown and sceptre), and Christ (with crossed nimbus and book of the Gospels). Inscr.: SEX ETATES SVNT MVNDI ("There are six ages of the world"), and YDRIA METRETAS CAPIENS EST QVELIBET ETAS. LIMPHA DAT HISTORIAM V'(*inum*) NOTAT ALLEGORIAM ("Any one of the ages is a waterpot containing firkins. The water gives the story, the wine signifies the allegory").

6 *The Six Ages of Man*, represented by a babe (INFANTIA), a boy with ball and curved stick (PVERITIA), a youth with a sceptre, perhaps for academic distinction (ADOLESCENTIA), a young man with sword (IVENTVS), a man with wallet and loaf (VIRILITAS), and a bald old man with a crutch (SENECTVS). Inscr.: SEX ETATES HOMINIS and PRIMVM SIGNORVM DEVS FACIENDO SVORVM IN VINVM MORVM CONVERTIT AQVAM VITIORVM ("By working the first of his signs God turned the water of vices into the wine of good morals").

The medallion has been pieced out with fragments of inscription from other, lost medallions: ATVR IN PACIO D MARIS RBRIS (*Unda maris rubri spacio divisa salubri*, "The wave of Red Sea divided by a safe space", signifying a mind purified from vice, a second type of the Baptism, with perhaps [*Baptiz*]*atur D*[*ominus*], "The Lord is baptized", possibly belonging to the lost Baptism medallion).

7 *The Miraculous Draught of Fishes*. Our Lord, with scroll, in a boat with SS. Peter and Andrew; SS. James and John (beardless) in another boat. All four draw a net from the broken meshes of which some of the fishes are escaping, realistically shown by painting partly on the inner, partly on the outer side of the glass. Inscr.: PISCATIO APL'ORVM (*Apostolorum*) VBI RETE RV̄PITVR("The fishing of the Apostles where the net breaks").

9   *St Peter* (S. PETRVS) *with the Church from among the Jews.*
    (ECCL'IA DE IVDEIS). On the right, two PHA-
    RISEI walk out of the domed church; St Peter, a crutch
    in his hand, sits on a platform above a crowd of
    converts. Inscr.: VERBVM RETE RATIS PETRI
    DOMVS HEC PIETATIS: PISCES IVDEI QVI
    RETE FORANT PHARISEI ("The word is the net;
    the boat of Peter is this house of piety; the Jewish fishes
    who make holes in the net are the Pharisees").

Two panels from Window VI

11 *The Gentiles.* Inscr.: SOLLICITE GENTES STANT
    VERBA DEI SITIENTES ("The Gentiles stand
    anxiously thirsting for God").
12 *The Pharisees*, incredulous. Inscr.: HI SVNT VERBA
    DEI QVI CONTEMPNVNT PHARISEI ("These
    are the Pharisees who despise the words of God").

NORTH CHOIR TRIFORIUM

THE three windows retain original armatures, borders, and
ground patterns of floral scrollwork, dating from about 1200.
In them have been inserted medallions, three in each, of about
the same date, with scenes from the lives of the sainted archbishops, Dunstan and Alphege; their original situation is pre-

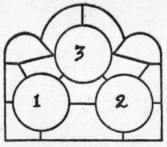

CHOIR TRIFORIUM, N. & S.

sumed to have been in the Choir Aisles in the first bays east of the eastern Transepts, close to the altars of the respective saints.

WINDOW I
(*St Dunstan*)

1   *King Edwy's release from Hell*, by the prayers of the saint. Dunstan, in mitre and vestments, beckons towards the king who is seen, crowned, among other figures amid flames emerging from the jaws of Hell; two other victims are being dragged by demons from clouds towards the gaping mouth.

2   *An Ordination scene* (perhaps Archbishop Odo ordaining Dunstan). The archbishop, in full vestments, stands before an altar on which are a chalice and a book; he extends his hand towards a chalice held by a kneeling priest. The interpretation of the subject is somewhat uncertain.

3   *Dunstan dividing the stricter Monks from the secular "Clerks"*, grouped on either side of him, turning to left and right respectively.

WINDOW II
(*St Dunstan*)

1   *The Saint's vision.* Our Lord appears among clouds between angels to Dunstan, asleep fully vested in bed; the angels hold a scroll with remains of an inscription.

2   *Dunstan and the Devil at Glastonbury.* The saint kneels before an altar; outside the church the Devil, with serpent-headed tail, flees before an angel. Despite intimidation by the Fiend, Dunstan came to the church to give thanks for recovery from illness; finding the door fastened, he climbed a ladder and was helped in through the roof by an angel.

3   *The Miracle of Calne.* During an argument with his adversaries in an upper room the floor gave way, Dunstan remaining unharmed whilst they were thrown

35

to the ground. He stoops to help a young man stepping up whilst another falls backward; behind, a group of armed opponents.

WINDOW III
(*St Alphege*)

1   *The Siege of Canterbury by the Danes.* Saxon defenders hurl stones at the assailants or thrust lances through them. Both forces are armed with helmets, chain mail, and shields similar to those in the Bayeux Tapestry.

2   *The Massacre of the Monks.* St Alphege, in mitre and chasuble, attacked by Danes with swords and a battle-axe whilst he blesses a falling monk; others lie prostrate; the severed head of one is rendered in pink glass with ruby "flash" blood-stains.

3   *Alphege carried off by the Danes.* He is being dragged on to a ship with dragon prow.

SOUTH CHOIR TRIFORIUM

THE windows are similar in disposition to those facing them on the north side. No. III retains its original 13th-century border; apart from this the borders and groundwork of all three windows were made up of contemporary fragments by S. C. Caldwell. The enclosed medallions in Windows I and III were originally in windows of the Apse Clerestory (see p. 17). Those in Window II, slightly later in date, were perhaps originally in one of the side chapels. All are in poor condition and considerably restored.

WINDOW I

1   *The Dormition of the Virgin.* She lies with eyes closed, surrounded by five of the Apostles.

2   *The Assumption.* Surrounded by angels, she rises through clouds, carrying the Infant Christ.

PLATE 3. CRYPT, EAST WINDOW, UPPER PART. ABOUT A.D. 1200.

facing p. 36

3   *The Coronation of the Virgin.* She sits holding a palm-
     branch facing our Lord, who crowns her; to left and
     right, angels with censers.

WINDOW II

1   *The Crucifixion.*
2   *The Resurrection.* Censing angels on either side of the
     risen Christ; a sleeping soldier in chain mail below.
3   *The Ascension.* The robe and feet of Christ are seen
     among clouds; the Virgin and six Apostles watch from
     below.

WINDOW III

1   *The Nativity.* St Joseph and the Virgin are watching
     over the Infant; an ox and an ass and a shepherd with
     a lamb stand behind; a lamp hangs above.
2   *The Adoration of the Magi.*
3   *The Presentation in the Temple.* Simeon and Anna on the
     right, St Joseph with two doves in a basket on the left;
     two candles on the altar.

CRYPT

EAST WINDOW

THE east window of the former Lady Chapel has always
retained its original border and had restored to it (in 1944) its
uppermost panel, brought from St Alban's Court, Nonington,
in 1938; these portions may be dated about 1200 or a little
earlier. The lower part of the window is divided into compart-
ments by horizontal bands of quatrefoil ornaments which were
probably originally in the Jesse Window (see p. 45). The
panel forming the compartment immediately below (No. 2)
is a recent reconstruction by S. C. Caldwell, partly in
13th-century glass, of a panel originally in the last of the

"Theological" windows (No. XII). The next compartment has been filled with early 13th-century panels (Nos. 3, 4) from a series of Patriarchs, Prophets, and Apostles which were, in 1794 and probably originally, in Petham Church, Kent, and not in the nave of the Cathedral as formerly stated by the author[1]; other panels of this series are now in the Water Tower (see p. 69).

Early French glass, as well as some quarries and other remnants of later glass, in other windows of the crypt are for convenience included here.

1   *The Virgin and Child.* The Virgin, crowned, sits on a throne; the Child on her knee holds the book of the Gospel and raises his right hand in benediction. On either side angels kneel on one knee, swinging censers; the dove of the Holy Ghost descends among clouds above the Virgin's head. The treatment of the subject may be compared with that in the "*Belle Verrière*" at Chartres. (Pl. 3).

2   *The Crucifixion.* Composed, partly with ancient glass, by S. C. Caldwell. The face and the loin-cloth of our Lord are ancient, as also portions of the background and of the draperies of the other figures.

3   *Jacob* and *Isaac*, with their names IACOBAS and ISAAC and scrolls inscribed respectively: [*Ex*] IVIT SONVS EORVM ("Their sound went into all the earth", Rom. 10. 18), and DICENT: OFFERENTÊ (*Benedicent offerentes* or *offerentem*).

4   *Isaiah* and *Jeremiah*, with their names ISAIAS and IEREMIAS and scrolls with defective inscriptions: PPREPERO DIC VE (deciphered by Professor Claude Jenkins as for *Praepropere dic ve*, "With all haste cry woe!") and ...S..SERVAT.

5   *Unidentified subject.* A man and woman coming out of a house to meet two young messengers. Inscr. (defective): ...CAVIT...CLESIA...DICI. Perhaps from one of the missing "Miracle" windows (see p. 47).

[1] See C. R. Councer in *Archaeologia Cantiana*, LXIII, 1950, p. 158.

ST GABRIEL'S CHAPEL

A window was filled (1955), as a gift from the Friends of Canterbury Cathedral, with French glass—14th-century *grisaille* surrounding a 13th-century medallion with an unidentified subject, apparently an anointing; a figure on the right holds a scroll inscribed: PANES.... The glass was formerly in the chapel of Costessey Hall, Norfolk.

SOUTH AISLE

The following late 15th-century glass has been inserted in a south aisle window of the Crypt, beneath the Choir. All but No. 4 are painted in black and silver-yellow stain.

1   *Heraldic Rose*. Medallion set in a lozenge made up of fragments with stems.
2   *Portcullis*, badge of the Tudors, introduced by Henry VII in 1485. Quarry set among foliage wiped out of a "smear" of grey.
3   *Rebus of Archbishop John Moreton* (1486–1501): an eagle (symbol of St John the Evangelist) wearing an archiepiscopal pallium, standing on a "ton" inscribed *mor*. Quarry set as No. 2.
4   *The Agnus Dei*, couched, holding a cross. Medallion set in a lozenge with foliage.

CORONA
EAST WINDOW

THE east window gives a brief summary in a single window of part of the theme set out at length in the windows of the Choir Aisles (see p. 23); it depicts in the five middle panels the Passion and Triumph of Christ, with corresponding Types from the Old Testament in the flanking medallions on either side. The subjects are to be read from the bottom of the window upwards. The interspaces between the panels are filled with tufts of foliage on scrolled stems, variously coloured, of outstanding beauty, in which can be recognized a notable advance from the Romanesque austerity of the earliest windows towards the lighter and more free treatment of early Gothic. A date in the first quarter of the 13th century seems likely. The window was restored by George Austin about 1853, when four panels were inserted, mostly or entirely in new glass (Nos. 1, 11, 12, 14).

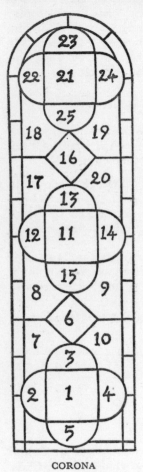

CORONA
EAST WINDOW

1   *The Crucifixion.* Modern, except for the blue background, the loin-cloth of Christ, and portions of other draperies.

2   *Moses striking the Rock*, type of wounding of the side of Christ. Men with bowls and sheep drink from the stream. Inscr.: HAVSTVS SPIC (for *sic*) PATITVR. LAPIS IS LATVS HIC APERITVR: EST AQVA CARNALI CRVOR AVTEM SPIRITVALI ("Just as this stone suffers the drawing [of water], so the side of this other is riven: water is for the carnal, but blood for the spiritual").

3   *The Offering of Isaac.* He lies on billets laid symbolically crosswise on the altar; Abraham kindles the fire with a torch, whilst the angel grasps the point of his sword; a ram in a thicket below.

4   *The Passover*. A man with a bowl marks with the sign
     T (*tau*), symbolizing the Cross, the lintel of a doorway,
     whilst two youths slay a lamb the blood of which,
     gushing into a bowl, stains the knife (in white glass,
     with a touch of ruby "flash" at the tip). Inscr.: LABE
     CARENS NAT*VS* ET AGNVS VT INMACVLATVS
     PECCATVM FACT'(*us*) PECCATORVM PIE
     TACTVS ("He that was born free from taint and as a
     spotless lamb was made the sin of sinners when
     smitten in piety").

5   *The Grapes of Eshcol*, type of Christ and Simon of
     Cyrene, and of the vintage of the Eucharistic wine,
     foretelling the Promised Land won by the Passion.
     The spies returning with the bunch of grapes. Inscr.:
     BOTRVM RESPICERE NEGAT HIC. SITIT ISTE
     VIDERE: ISRAEL IGNORAT CHRISTVM: GEN-
     TILIS ADORAT ("This one refuses to look back at
     the cluster, the other thirsts to see it; Israel knows not
     Christ, the Gentile adores him"). Partly restored.

6   *The Entombment*. Two men lower the body of Christ into
     a marble sarcophagus; a third, perhaps St Joseph of
     Arimathaea, pours ointment from a flask. The two
     Marys stand behind. A tree grows on the rock summit
     of the sepulchre.

7   *Joseph in the Pit* (the *cisterna* of the Vulgate), which his
     brethren, with mattocks, are filling; one of them holds
     his coat. The hand of God issues from a cloud above, to
     foretell deliverance. Inscr. (mutilated): ARTAT TE
     C*PITVR PAR*VLVS PVERVM LACVS IST *OR
     SIGNA* FICAT CRISTVM PVER...MVL*M*...
     ISTVM ("The tomb confines thee, O Christ, this pool
     the boy: the boy signifies Christ and the pool this
     tomb"). The first italicized portions belong to No. 9,
     to which the missing portion *riste tum* has been trans-
     ferred; the last part should read: ...*iste: significat
     Cristum puer et tumulum lacus istum*.

8   *Samson and Delilah*. They lie in bed, whilst Philistines
     (in helmets with nasal and chain mail) stand outside a

door. Inscr.: ECCLESIE CAVSA C*HRIS*TI CARO MARMORE CLAVSA: VT SAMSON TIPICE CAVSA DORMIVIT AMICE ("For the sake of the Church the flesh of Christ was shut in the marble, just as Samson typically slept for the sake of his beloved").

9   *Jonah cast into the Sea.* A "great fish" receives the prophet with open jaws as he is lowered out of the ship. Inscr. (defective): TENTVS ET EXTRVSVS. ABSORPTVS. PISCE RECLVSVS: HIC *RISTE-TVME PITVR PARITER* MORITVR SEPELITVR; this should read: ...*hic Cristus capitur pariter*...: the italicized portions are partly an insertion from No. 7, partly a modern restoration ("He is held and thrust out, swallowed, shut up in the fish; here in like manner Christ is taken, dies, and is buried").

10   *Daniel in Babylon.* The prophet, mitred, in a walled pit, inscribed DANIEL; behind, a city with the name BABILONIA. Inscr.: CLAVSTRA LEO PATITVR DANIEL. CRIST'(*us*) SEPELITVR: HVNC LEO NON TANGIT NECIS ILLE REPAGVLA FR-ANGIT ("The prison; the lion; Daniel suffers; Christ is buried; this man the lion does not touch, this other breaks the bars of death").

11   *The Resurrection.* Christ stepping from the tomb. Mostly modern.

12   *Noah.* Except the title: NOE IN ARCHA, a modern copy of North Choir Aisle, III 8.

14   *Michal and David.* Modern.

15   *Moses and the Burning Bush.* He walks with three sheep towards the bush above which the head of the Almighty issues from a cloud.

16   *The Ascension.* The Apostles and the Virgin look up as our Lord disappears among clouds. Nos. 17–20 are the corresponding types.

17   *The High Priest entering the Holy of Holies.* He kneels with a censer before the mercy-seat; above it two Cherubim ("Righteousness and Peace", Ps. 85. 10) kissing each other. Another priest stands outside the veil of the

42

Temple. Inscr. (mutilated): TVRBAEOSSTAM...
NTVAT...REDITHE. CRDEAMVS.

18   *The Ascension of Elijah.* He kneels in a chariot whilst
his cloak is wafted towards Elisha: the horses partly
hidden in a cloud. Fourteenth-century oak-leaves
inserted. Inscr. (defective): RAPT...TEGMEN EO
DAT HELIAS HOC HEL...MORTE ("When he
had been carried away Elias gave this garment to
Eliseus").

19   *The Sundial of Ahaz* (Isa. 38. 8). Isaiah stands by the
sick-bed of Hezekiah (who wears a crown); above are
a semicircular dial and the red sun. Inscr. (defective):
DENIS ACCEDENS GRADIB'(*us*) SOL...TQ...S
EGR...ILLVC [QV'?] REGRESSVS. (...*sol atque
regressus*..., "The sun going up by ten degrees and
returning...returning thither").

20   *The Translation of Enoch.* He is shown twice, on the right
in prayer, his name ENOCH appended, on the left
ascending towards a cloud. Inscr.: ENOCH SVB-
LATVS ET ADHVC IN CARNE MORATVS: HIC
ASCENSVRVS FVIT HVC IVDEX RED[I]TVRVS
("Enoch was taken up and hitherto remained in the
flesh: He [Christ] was about to ascend, to return hither
as judge").

21, 23 *Christ in Majesty* and *Pentecost*. He is enthroned on a
rainbow (Rev. 4. 3) between adoring angels, his right
hand raised in benediction, a book in his left. From a
cloud beneath his feet eleven crimson streams of fire
pour down upon the heads of the Apostles below. The
head of Christ and several others restored. Inscr.
(defective): PONT'(*us*) TERRA *VBDIAT REX TV
ATIENTI SE HOSTIA*. SOL'(*us*) AB ETERNO
CREO CVNCTA CREATA GVBERNO ("...alone
from eternity I create all things and govern
creation"). This part of the window has fairly close
parallels in the *Apocalypse* window at Bourges, and at
Poitiers.

43

22   *The Consecration of Aaron and his Sons.* Aaron kneels before Moses (MOYSES), who is setting a mitre on his head; behind, two figures already mitred; among the congregation below, a man with a basket of unleavened bread (Lev. 7. 2, 26). Inscr.: IN CAPVD HOC PRIMV(*m*) PER BARBAM FLVXIT IN IMV(*m*) QVOD PRI'(*us*) HIS *DAT I*DEM DAT NOBIS MODO PLENIVS IDEM (referring to Ps. 133. 2, "This first poured on his head flowed down over his beard"; the remainder translated by Dr Mason: "The same now gives to us that same which he before gave to these").

24   *Moses and Jethro* (Ex. 18. 13–24). [MOYS]ES sitting in judgement above the people, JETHRO beside him. Inscr. (defective) beginning: HIS EST DE CELO MOYSIS DA... ("To these Moses was given from heaven...").

25   *Moses receiving the Tables of the Law.* He kneels on the flaming mountain-top to take the Tables from the Almighty; a cloud separates him from the Israelites. Inscr. (partly disordered): NVBE TENEBRANTE LEX SPIRIT'(*us*) IGNE MICANTE CCELANS HI EST DAT' HE COCCLAT REVELANS ("In darkening cloud and flashing fire the law is the spirit"); Dr Mason thus interprets the rest: *Lex est hec celans datur hic occulta revelans* ("This law is one that conceals; here a law is given that reveals what is hidden").

"JESSE" WINDOW

The scheme of the "Tree of Jesse", illustrating the descent of Christ through David from Jesse, based on Isa. 11. 1–3, was first embodied in glass-painting in 1144, at St Denis, in a window now much restored, which for long remained the standard for similar windows wherever the Gothic style prevailed. The window at Canterbury in the Corona next to the east window on the north was designed as a Jesse window

PLATE 4. KING JOSIAH, FROM THE "TREE OF JESSE". EARLY
13TH CENTURY. CORONA. P. 44.

by George Austin in 1861, in imitation of surviving remnants of a 13th-century window which are shown by their style to be contemporary with the East Window. Bands of ornament from this Jesse window have been inserted in the east window of the Crypt (see p. 37).

In 1954 two panels from the original window, now inserted in the window adjacent to Austin's copy, were recovered by the bequest of Dr Philip Nelson. They came originally above the figure of Jesse. They had been removed in 1853 by George Austin from the places in which they had been set in 1780 to fill gaps in the East Window left by the destruction, in 1642, of the *Crucifixion* and the *Resurrection* in that window.[1] They depict respectively the Virgin (SCA MARIA) and King Josiah (IOSIAS) (Pl. 4); both are seated, with hands extended to grasp the leafy branches which spring symmetrically from the "stem of Jesse"; the arrangement is thus exactly parallel to that of St Denis, Chartres, and the panel surviving from the 12th-century "Jesse" at York Minster. It will be noticed that the figures, unlike those at St Denis and Chartres, have their names appended; they were originally flanked by half-quatrefoil medallions each containing a figure of a prophet.

SOUTH WINDOW

In this window has been inserted an early 13th-century panel bought in 1938 at St Alban's Court, Nonington, originally in all probability in Petham Church, near Canterbury.[2] Its subject is *Christ in Majesty*, his right hand raised in benediction, his left supporting a book. The figure is enclosed in a vesica-shaped aureole surrounded by the Emblems of the Evangelists—the angel (MATTHEVS), winged lion (MARCVS), winged ox (LVCAS), and eagle (IOHANNES); the inscriptions on the scrolls they hold (BINI, SIBIS, *UN*IT, FONT) have not been explained.

[1] Information of Mr S. C. Caldwell.
[2] So conjectured by Mr C. R. Councer, *Archaeologia Cantiana*, LXIII 1950, p. 158; probably not, as formerly stated, in the Cathedral.

NORTH-EAST TRANSEPT

WEST SIDE

MODERN. Scenes from the *Old Testament*. In memory of Lord Kingsdown (d. 1867). By Clayton and Bell.

ST MARTIN'S CHAPEL

The window is filled with ornament within a border of 13th-century glass (partly restored): set in this groundwork are five roundels of which four are modern and only the nethermost, described below, is made up out of glass of the 13th century with considerable restorations.

> *St Martin and the Beggar*. The saint (S. MARTHMVS (*sic*)), nimbed, is dividing his cloak with the almost naked beggar. The inscription, parts of the beggar's figure and of the saint's drapery, the head and hindquarters of the horse are modern.

ST STEPHEN'S CHAPEL

MODERN. *Life of St Stephen*. Memorial to Archbishop Lord Lang of Lambeth. By John Baker, 1956.

SOUTH-EAST TRANSEPT

MODERN. Four windows in the south and east walls of this Transept are being filled with glass from designs by Erwin Bossanyi; one of these, depicting *God the Father of all Races*, was inserted in 1956.

ST JOHN'S CHAPEL

MODERN. "*Jesse*" window in 13th-century style, nearly duplicating that by the same artist in the Corona. Signed: "George Austin dicavit 1852".

ST GREGORY'S CHAPEL

MODERN. Scenes from the *Life of Christ*. Signed: "George Austin dicavit 1852".

TRINITY CHAPEL AISLE

ALL twelve windows of the ambulatory have their original iron armatures. Nos. 3–7, 11, 12 retain some or all of the glass originally belonging to them; only two others (Nos. 1, 9) contain ancient glass inserted in recent times, consisting partly of medallions which originally belonged to windows of this series, partly of modern compositions made up to a large extent out of ancient fragments. The surviving windows illustrate the miracles as recorded to have taken place through the intercessions of St Thomas of Canterbury or the healing virtue of his blood in the years immediately following his murder. It was previously surmised as probable, and has only lately become evident, that the first window in the series was intended as a prelude to the miracle stories filling the remainder; it was devoted to the saint's martyrdom and perhaps also earlier incidents in his life, such as those still to be seen depicted in windows only slightly earlier in date at Sens and Chartres Cathedrals. The miracle incidents have in many cases been identified by reference to detailed accounts set down soon after the murder by two monks of Christ Church— Benedict, later Prior of Canterbury and eventually Abbot of Peterborough, and William.

The windows are composed of "medallions" varying in form from window to window, set among foliage or trellis-work within an outer border; their general disposition is closely similar to those of Chartres (of which Becket's secretary, John of Salisbury, became Bishop) and Sens. They are the work of several glass-painters, not all of equal merit. No. 5 has a foliage background of singular distinction, No. 4 may be noted for the fine diapering of the medallions. These windows are valuable not only for their beauty but also as evidence of the appearance of the saint's shrine and tomb and as illustrations of the daily life of their time—its furniture, tools, weapons, etc.

WINDOW I

This window has always retained its original border. The remainder is made up partly of scraps of ancient glass, with the painted trace-lines in some cases restored by S. C. Caldwell, partly of modern glass.[1] At the foot of the windows has been inserted a figure of St Thomas, reassembled from fragments taken out of the North Choir Aisle Triforium windows, which is credibly believed originally to have occupied a triforium window in the Eastern Transept, presumably near the altar of St Thomas; it is earlier than the remainder of the window and may be dated about 1200. Of the remaining panels, most are imaginary reconstructions of incidents in the life of the saint. No. 1, at the apex of the window, almost certainly belonged originally where it has now been placed. Of another (No. 7) enough remains in ancient glass to show that it depicted Becket's three murderers breaking in at the cathedral door; it therefore always belonged to the window and gives the clue to the original subject of the whole—the life of the saint. The most recently recovered medallion (No. 12, with much ancient glass) is especially interesting because of its subject and the "mock Arabic" inscription (compare p. 26). Five of the medallions, Nos. 2, 6, 10, 11, and 14, with scenes relating to the miracles, belonged to one of the other windows in the series, from which the rest of the ancient glass has been lost.

1   *St Thomas Becket* enthroned and vested as Archbishop, in the act of benediction (the face modern).
2   *An offering of a coil of wire at the tomb of the saint.*
3   *Laymen at an altar.*
4   *King Henry II and Becket.*
5   *Clerics at an altar.*

[1] See *Friends of Canterbury Cathedral, 27th Annual Report,* 1954, p. 14.

48

PLATE 5. ARCHBISHOP BECKET APPEARING IN A DREAM TO KING LOUIS VII. 13TH CENTURY. TRINITY CHAPEL, WINDOW IV. P. 52.

6   *Unidentified*, perhaps a pilgrim who has fainted on the way.

7   *Becket's murderers at the Cathedral door*; the chain mail and helmet of the foremost knight, also much of the door with its decorative hinge-irons, are ancient.

8   *The Archbishop at the altar.*

9   *One of the knights and a monk.*

10, 14   *Victory in a judicial combat.* (10) Two young men, cross-gartered, fighting, with shields and cudgels; the judge with staff on the left. Inscr.: PVGNANT PVGILES MAG... ("The fighters fight with great [fury?]").
(14) The stronger lifts his opponent on his back, to dash him, imploring the aid of St Thomas, to the ground; shields and cudgels lie discarded. The judge advances. Inscr.: MINOR DESPERATVS S$\overline{\text{CM}}$ TH. INVOCAT ("The smaller man in despair calls upon St Thomas").

11   *A sick man.*

12   *King Henry II doing penance* at the tomb of Becket.

13   *An offering at the tomb.*

15   *A cripple at the tomb*, a child in a tight bonnet carried on a man's back. Inscr. defective.

16   *St Thomas*, vested in mitre, chasuble, pall, dalmatic, and alb. Inscr.: S.THOMA..E(*piscopus*). (See above.)

WINDOW III

Panels 4 and 7 were reinstated where they now are after having been removed in 1792 by Dean Powys to the South-west Transept.

1-3   *A riding-accident*, perhaps Baldric injured by a fall from his horse. (1) A man seizing a restive horse whilst another comes to the help of the fallen rider. Inscr. defective. (3) Urged by his wife, he invokes St Thomas, who appears to him in his sleep. Inscr. fragmentary. (2) He gives thanks, bare-legged, at the tomb; his shoes are on the ground. Inscr. fragmentary.

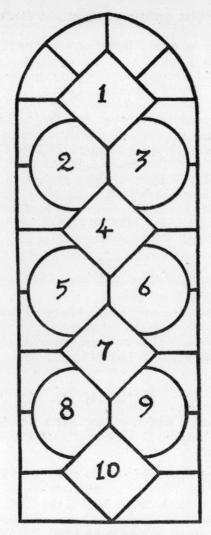

TRINITY CHAPEL III

4   *Stephen of Hoylake* delivered from nightmares. Three
       demons surround him, a veiled woman soothes him.
       Inscr. (defective): VEXAT...EIONIO.

5-7   *Pilgrimage scenes.* (5) Four pilgrims on horseback, four
       walk behind, in front a cripple on crutches to whom one
       of the riders seems to be giving a ring. (6) Five pilgrims
       at St Thomas's Well (possibly those saved by the saint
       from shipwreck on their way to Compostella, with bags
       containing crosses for St James which they gave to St
       Thomas); a woman drinks, others carry embroidered
       bags; a priest in attendance holding a cup and a bag;
       a cup on a shelf. (7) A tomb (not recognisably that of
       St Thomas) with figures grouped round it.

8   *A vision by night,* possibly the graceful youth appearing
       to William Patrick, who was racked with toothache,
       and healing him with a touch of St Thomas's cloak.

9   *William the Priest, of London,* cured of palsy by drinking
       a drop of the Saint's blood at the tomb; the blood is
       distilled by a monk with a long spoon out of a bottle
       into a cup of water poured by another monk from a
       flask. Inscr. (defective): SANG(*uis*) DIS(*tillatus*?)
       EOIN AQVA: [WIL]LELMVS SACERDOS LVN-
       DON'(*ensis*) ("William the priest of London").

10   *A cure at the tomb*; a monk touching the eyes of a youth,
       a man with pains in the head waiting his turn, a
       woman pressing her hand against her cheek.

WINDOW IV

The medallions are noteworthy for the splendid diaper,
varying in composition, of foliage and berries on coiled stems
in reserve on the blue ground (paralleled at Lincoln and
Strasburg); for the "crown" ornament surrounding them see
p. 26.

1   *Pilgrims with water of St Thomas*; the water mixed with
       blood is represented by pink glass flashed with ruby.
       Inscr. (fragmentary, belonging elsewhere): *SVBTPE-
       SHRE VESTIS: PERO EST BACVLS.*

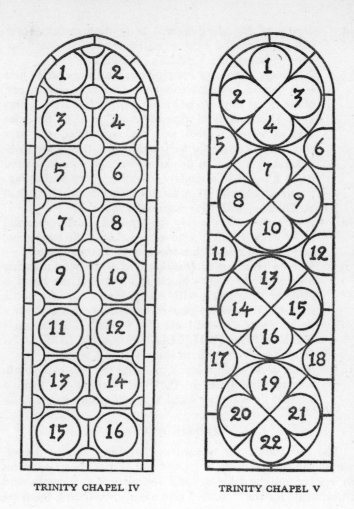

TRINITY CHAPEL IV   TRINITY CHAPEL V

2   *St Thomas visiting a sick man.* Inscr.: QVA DOLET HAC PLANAT DOLET HIS TRIB'(*us*) ET TRIA SANAT ("Where the pain is, there he smooths; the pain is in three places, and he heals the three").

3, 4   *The healing of Petronilla, an epileptic nun of Polesworth.* (3) She is brought in a fit to her abbess. Inscr. (defective): CONVALET EGRO *EFVNCT* ("She grows better, she is sick..."). (4) Her feet are being bathed near the tomb, on which are two lighted candles; behind it, a monk with a spoon and bowl, and a man pouring holy water into a bowl held by a woman. Inscr. (defective): S:DE*MIMPHATV*NONGIN CHOTA (*lympha*, the healing water).

5, 6, 7 Modern.

8   *The Dream of Louis VII, King of France.* St Thomas appears to the king (who wears his crown in bed), warning him to make a pilgrimage to Canterbury if he wishes his ailing son to get better. Louis visited the tomb in 1179 with gifts including the "régale" of France. Inscr. (defective): ELLAM *MRADI*VARIAN (?)SFV. Patched with 15th-century foliage. (Pl.5).

9, 10 *Healing of Robert of Cricklade, Prior of St Frideswide's Oxford.* (9) Suffering from swollen feet he totters to the tomb; a priest receives him. Inscr. (defective): CLINICVS EN *REDDEVCEMI* VNVS SARCINA SERVIS ("The physician...the bundle to the servants"). (10) His thanksgiving at the tomb, casting off his boots, cloak, and stick. Inscr.: EST BACVLVS VESTIS PERO CVRE SIBI TESTIS ("His stick, his garment, his boot are witness to him of his cure").

11, 12 *Cure of a woman* (perhaps Juliana Puintel). (11) St Thomas appears, pointing her to his tomb. Inscr.: VISCERE TORQVÆTVR CITAT HIC OFFERRE IVBEVTR (*sic*) ("She is tormented in her bowels, he summons her, she is bidden to make an offering"). (12) She offers a coil of wire. Inscr.: EXILIT A SOMNIS OFFERT DOLOR EXCIDIT OMN*ITV*

("She leaps up from her sleep and makes an offering; all the pain falls away").

13, 14 *Cure of a maniac* (perhaps Henry of Fordwich). (13) He is being thrust by men with birch-rods towards the tomb on which are a money-box and coils of wire. Inscr.: AMENS ACCEDIT ("He approaches, demented"). (14) The cured sufferer kneels at the tomb, cord and birch-rods on the ground. Inscr.: ORAT SANVSQ' RECEDIT ("He prays and goes back healed").

15, 16 *Audrey of Canterbury*, cured of quartan fever. (15) She is about to drink from a bowl offered by a priest. Inscr.: ARVIT EXANGVIS REDIT HVASTO SANGVINE SANGVIS ("She was dried up, bloodless; when the blood [of St Thomas] had been imbibed, her blood came back"). (16) She advances whilst a priest mixes a draught with a spoon; between them a man with a flask, who is perhaps explaining that the martyr's blood must be mixed with water. Inscr.: CESSANT QUARTANE VIS FORMA SVBIT QVASI SANE ("The quartan fevers depart, her strength, her figure, come back as in health").

WINDOW V

A date about 1220 is indicated by the representation of the shrine of St Thomas in the first panel.

1   *St Thomas appearing to a sleeping monk*. His archiepiscopal cross in hand, he issues from the end of his shrine, which shows its original form before the addition of a third finial by Prior Henry of Eastry, in 1315. The defective inscription ends with FERETRO ("shrine"). The pattern on the shrine may be compared with that of many Limoges enamel reliquaries. The sleeper is perhaps one of the chroniclers of the miracles, William of Canterbury or Benedict of Peterborough, whom the saint is prompting.

2   Perhaps *Roger of Valognes* cured of a swollen foot, which an attendant is bathing. Inscr. (defective): DETV-MET IN VOTO LAVACRO...SANGVINE... ("As he makes his vow, washes, and drinks the blood, the swelling goes down").

3   *A woman at the tomb.* She draws up her gown to reveal a green stocking; a monk blesses her. Inscr.: MAGNI-FICAT G*VNTA* RATVM LETVM MEDICVM MEDICATVS ("The healed sufferer glorifies the joyful healer"); in view of the masculine *medicatus* this inscription is perhaps out of place and belonged to one of the missing original panels of the window. Note the dragon-ornaments on the roof-beam.

4   *Godwin of Boxgrove*(?). A man, nearly naked, receiving a shirt from another; on the right, a priest pointing to a book on a lectern and the tomb of St Thomas. Perhaps originally two panels, combined in a restoration. Inscr. (introduced from another panel, now missing): GVSTAT DISTENTA CVTE FIT GVSTV ME[DICA] TV[S] ("His skin distended, he tastes, by the tasting he is cured"); this perhaps relates to a cure of dropsy or leprosy of which the charitable act depicted in this panel may be the sequel. Probably Godwin of Boxgrove, who gave away his clothes, to be an example of voluntary poverty, in response to a dream of St Thomas taking off his robe; the scene on the right perhaps relates to Matthew 25. 36 ("Clothing the naked").

5, 6   *A woman with dropsy visits the tomb.* (5) The sufferer, with a crutch and a companion to support her, approaches a building. Inscr.: QVE VENIT EGROTA TVR-GESCIT YDROPICA TOTA ("She who comes sick is all swollen with dropsy"). (6) They depart, looking back. Inscr. (in disorder): GREM*D*ITFLATA*RE*... VENERAT IN ATENVATA ("She had come with bosom swollen, she returns attenuated").

7–9 Modern.

10–12 *The lame daughters of Godbold of Boxley.* (11) The sisters, lame from birth, approach the Cathedral on crutches. Inscr.: NATE SORTE PARI PEREGRE VENIVNT MEDICAR[I] ("Born with an equal lot they come on pilgrimage to be cured"). (10) The elder visited by St Thomas while asleep at the tomb over which the younger leans on crutches. Inscr. (defective): DESAN-*STAN*..GA SOROR...ANXIA..ESE. (12) The saint appears to the weeping younger sister whilst the elder gives thanks. Inscr. (wrongly re-set): SANAT MAIORE[M] [N]OX PRIMA SEDA' *(secunda)* MIN-OREM ("The first night brings health to the elder, the second to the younger"). The younger was healed on appealing to the saint in the words of Esau (Gen. 27. 38).

13–18 *Eilward of Westoning* and his quarrel with Fulk, from whom he stole a pair of ditcher's gloves and a whetstone, to make good an undischarged debt. (14) Eilward brought before the magistrate. Inscr. (disordered and defective): PIGNVS IAM*MO* DICIVM VM CEN-SETVR INIQVVM ("He is sentenced to a pledge, judgment, and an unjust penalty *(damnum)*"); *pignus* perhaps refers to the ordeal by water he was made to undergo. (15) His punishment, by blinding and mutila-tion, in the presence of the magistrate. Inscr. (defec-tive): *ADVNTVR* ECTA SVNT LVMINA MEMBRA RESECTA ("His eyes are cut out, his members amputated"). (17) Eilward in bed, healed by St Thomas, who makes the Sign of the Cross over him with his pastoral staff. Inscr. (defective): REDDITA SVCCRE[SCVNT] *FVRTVM BE* SENSIMQ' RE-CRESCVNT ("...are restored and gradually swell up again"). (16) He points to his eyes whilst pilgrims with a money-bag offer him silver coins and he gives a gold coin to a crippled beggar, who supports himself with his hands on iron clogs. Inscr. (defective): AM

NST*OR*TEM VA SINISTRA (the last word may refer to his giving alms with his left hand). (18) He gives thanks at the tomb. Inscr.: ASTAT NARRANTI POPVLVS MAGNALIA SANCTI ("The people stand by as he narrates the mighty works of the saint"). (13) Probably a scene from another story, perhaps *Gerald, a knight of " Porta Clausa"* or *Walter of Lisors*, who were cured of leprosy—a man riding in and out of the city. Inscr. (defective): SPE RECREANTE PR.. *TADN* T ADEVNTI' LEPRA RECEDIT ("Hope creating him afresh, he prays (*precat?*); as he approaches his leprosy abates").

19–21   *The cellarer Hugh of Jervaulx.* (19) The Abbot of Jervaulx administering extreme unction to his dying monk. Inscr.: DES[P]ERANT MEDICI PATER & FRATRES & AMICI ("The physician, his father and brothers and friends are in despair"). (20) The Abbot gives him a draught of water from the holy well. Inscr.: SPES DESPERANTI SVPEREST IN SANGVINE SANCTI *IME* ("Hope remains for the hopeless in the blood of the saint"). (21) Hugh cured by a discharge of blood; a man in a skull-cap, perhaps a lay physician, among the onlookers. Inscr. (defective): ...SC BIBIT HIC CVIS SANGVINE SANAT ("...drinks... heals with the blood").

22   Modern.

WINDOW VI

1–3   *Juliana of Rochester* cured of her blindness. (1) She is led with closed eyes by her father, Gerard. Inscr.: ...AT *EGRVM E* TRAHITVR PEREGRE SINE LVCE ("She is led [by her father] on her pilgrimage, without light"). (2) As she leans, supported by her father, over the tomb, a priest touches her eyes with water from a bowl; two lamps hang above. Inscr.: HIC CRVOR EST TACTVS S'(*ed*) NONDVM [L]ANGVOR ABA[CTVS, displaced by *MA*] ("Here the blood [of St Thomas] is applied, but the weakness is not yet

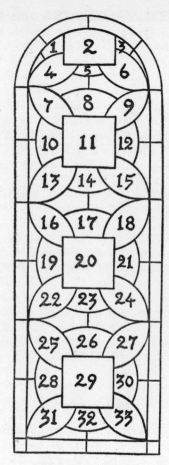

TRINITY CHAPEL VI

removed"). (3) Sitting by her father, she points to her eyes, now seeing. Inscr.: SANA DOMI FACTA LVX REDDITA CVRA PERACTA ("At home she is made whole, the light is given back [to her eyes], the cure is completed").

4–9 *Richard Sunieve of Egewerde* (Edgworth), cured of leprosy. (4) He drives to pasture the horses of his master, Richard Fitzhenry; in his left hand a short post and cord for tethering them. Inscr.: PASTOR ALEN-DORVM CVRAM PVER EGIT EQVORVM ("The boy herdsman performed the task of feeding the horses"). (5) He sleeps beneath a bush, to awake a leper, whilst the horses browse, the cord wound as a girth round the nearest. Inscr.: SANVS SOPITVR LEPRA SVRGENS OPERITVR ("He falls asleep healthy, when he rises he is covered with leprosy"). (6) He sits up in bed to take food offered on a tray at arm's length by his mother, her mouth muffled against infection. Inscr.: OMNIB; ABIECTVS VIX SIC A MATRE REFECTVS ("Cast out by all he is thus scarcely fed by his mother"). (7) Now healed, he prostrates himself before the tomb, feeling his face; a priest drops blood of the saint (represented by a piece of ruby glass) with a rod into a bowl. Inscr.: LAN-GVIDVS ERIGITVR VENIT ORAT POTAT ABIVIT ("He rises languid, he comes, prays, drinks, goes away"). (8) Followed by his mother, he shows his face, now healed, to his master and mistress. Inscr.: FIT CARO QVE PRIDEM COLOR & VIGOR & STATVS IDEM ("His flesh becomes as before, his complexion and strength and carriage are the same"). (9) In the presence of his mother and employers he offers money at the tomb. Inscr. (defective): AMATER DOMVS SVA TOTA ("...his whole household"). (Pl. 6).

10–12 Modern; some ancient ruby in No. 12.

13–15 *Robert of Rochester*, the boy drowned in the Medway whilst stoning frogs. (13) Boys throwing stones at frogs leaping out of the river, into which Robert falls face forwards. Inscr.: DVM RVIT *SN* FVNVS RANARVM CORRVIT VNVS ("As he rushes to kill the frogs one boy falls in"). (14) Two of his companions breathlessly report the accident to his parents. Inscr.: DEFVNCTVM FLENTES PISCANTVR IN AMNE P(*ar*)ENTES ("Weeping, the parents fish up the dead boy in the river").

16–18 Modern.

19–21 *The healing of the maniac* (probably a murderess. Matilda of Cologne). (19) Two men belabouring her with rods. Inscr. (displaced): ALTERNAT GESTVM NVNC VM NSA .. CQ' MOLESTVM ("She alternates her bearing, now sane, and [now] troublesome"). (20) She collapses beside the tomb of St Thomas under the blows of her attendants; to the right, a monk reading. Inscr.: STAT MODO IOCVNDA MODO LAPSA IACET MORIBVNDA ("Now she stands gleefully, now she collapses and lies as if dying"). (21) The victim prostrate at the tomb, on which a cowled priest is putting a candle. Inscr. (defective): AMEN CLAMAT AREDIT ADSVASA ("Amen is the cry, [she] returns [safe *or* sane] to her affairs").

22–24 Modern.

25–33 *The plague in the house of Sir Jordan Fitzeisulf*, of Pontefract (a friend of Becket). (31) The funeral of the first victim, the nurse Britonis: the coffin under a pall carried on a bier by four men, a priest in embroidered stole, with holy-water sprinkler, walking in front. Inscr.: NVT-RICIS FVNVS RELIQVIS SVA FLAGRA MINATVR ("The funeral of the nurse threatens the survivors with each his own scourge"). (32) Death of Sir John's son William, aged ten; the parents stoop over his bier which a priest is sprinkling with holy water. Inscr.: PERCVTITVR PVER & MORITVR PLANCTVS GEMINATVR ("The boy is smitten and dies, the lamentation is redoubled"). (33) Pilgrims arriving with water of St Thomas. The child's mother

60

lifts his head while Jordan pours water into his mouth. Inscr.: VOX PATRIS VIS MARTIRIS VT RESTI-TVATVR ("The voice of the father, the power of the martyr plead that he may be restored"). (25) Jordan receiving from his wife coins brought in a bowl and about to place two in each hand of the child, to be presented to the saint at Mid Lent. Inscr. (defective): PROFERT AD F[V]NS *S*VOTIVM CVN PRECE MVN' ("He brings to the corpse a votive gift with a prayer"). (26) The child sits up and feeds, the parents face to face at the bed-ends giving thanks. Inscr.: HIC PVER ERIGITVR SANVS NEC MARTIR ADITVR ("Here the boy rises healed, but no approach is made to the martyr"). (27) St Thomas, cross in hand, appearing to a sleeping leper named Gimp and bidding him to warn Jordan of what would happen if he failed to perform his vow. Inscr. (defective): ..*RO*.. [M]ANDATVR VOTI REVS VT NON EATVR ("Bound by his vow, he is commanded that the journey should not be made"). (28) The parents come to Gimp, who rises up to give his message. Inscr. (defective): [CR]EDVLVS ACCEDIT VOT*AMVN-DVM R* EC OBED *NAR* ("He approaches believingly, [he remembers] his vow and does not obey"; the missing parts of *voti meminit nec* conjectured by Dr Mason). (29) The leper's message having been ignored, an elder son of Jordan now dies; St Thomas armed with a sword above a corpse and mourners too ill to rise from their chairs. Inscr.: VINDICTE MOLES DOMVS EGRA & MORTVA PROLES ("The piling up of vengeance, a sick house and offspring dead"). (30) The vow accomplished. Jordan empties gold and silver coins on the tomb, followed by his wife and their boy with pilgrim's staves. Inscr. defective.

WINDOW VII

Of the sixteen medallions the upper (Nos. 1–8) were made up of miscellaneous fragments, including parts of inscriptions, by Samuel Caldwell, Senior, in 1893. Nos. 9–14 were brought from windows of the South Choir Aisle Triforium and Nos. 15 and 16 from windows facing these, in 1920. It will be noted that the inscriptions are in prose, not in the customary hexameter verse.

1   A man in bed, a priest, and others.

2   A woman making an offering at the tomb of St Thomas.

3, 4   Similar to No. 2.

5   A monk and others at the tomb. Inscr.: [V]ERBA DEI ("The words of God"), perhaps originally in Window VI of the Theological series (see p. 23).

6   Washing of feet at the tomb.

7   Figures at the tomb.

8   A man in bed drinking from a flask.

9–12   *William of Kellett* (near Lancaster), a carpenter who had been remiss in the performance of a vow. (9) His axe has slipped and cut his shin as he works at his open-air bench; clouds above, blood on the ground. Inscr.: (defective): D[V]M OPERATVR *NTV* AMSEC*NET*. EGROT .. T (.. *suram secat et egrotat*, "Whilst at work he cuts his shin and sickens"). (10) St Thomas, with pastoral staff, appears to him in a dream. Inscr. defective, and made up, comprising perhaps (*sangui*)-NEM SA(*ncti T*)HOME ("The blood of St Thomas") and (*vul*)NERATVS ("Wounded"). (11) A woman removes the bandage from his leg. Inscr.: LIGA-TVRAM SOLVIT & VVLNVS NON REPPIT ("She loosened the bandage and found no wound"). (12) Axe in hand and two more in his girdle William leaves Canterbury exultant for the open country. Inscr. (defective): EGRESSVS . AD OPA (*opera*) S *ESORAS*...*OMENDA* ("Going forth to work...".)

13–16   *Adam the forester* who was shot by a poacher. (13) To the left, with a companion carrying an axe, Adam trans-fixed through the throat by an arrow shot by one of two poachers on the right; the second walks away with a deer on his back. Inscr.: FVR FVGIENS GVTTVR PFORAT INSEQVENTIS ("The thief as he flies pierces the throat of his pursuer"). (14) A man in bed drinking from a glass flask watched by a man and woman (it is not certain that this medallion belongs to the story of the forester). Inscr.: BIBENS AQVAM S.*(ancti)* TH.*(omae)* SANVS EFFIC *MO* VA (*efficitur aqua*, "Drinking the water of St Thomas he is made whole by the water"). (15) Three friends visiting a sick man. Inscr. (defective): DESPERANT M *ON MBRI* ITER ERES AMICI (referring to friends and despair). (16) Adam's thank-offering at the tomb. Inscr. (mutilated): SIM MELOR MEDICO PRECES & MVNERA (". . . to the physician prayers and gifts").

WINDOW IX

Two medallions at the foot reinstated by S. C. Caldwell in 1929; the rest missing.

1 *Pilgrims on the road to Canterbury.*
2 *An offering at the tomb.*

WINDOW XI

Ancient glass, mostly reinstated by Samuel Caldwell, Senior, in memory of Anne (d. 27 December 1906) second wife of Canon Edward Moore, D.D. Medallions 1 and 4 were introduced later (1920) from the South Choir Aisle Triforium.

1–4 *John, the Groom of Roxburgh*, rescued from drowning in the Tweed. (1) His horse is being pulled out of the river into which he has been thrown. Inscr. (defective) including . . . A PLEBE REDVCTVS (". . . brought back by the people"). (2) Having been rescued by St Thomas, the groom crawls along a bridge, with water gushing from his mouth. Inscr. (defective) ending in . . ŌTE REPT' (perhaps *ponte repentem*, "crawling on the bridge"). (3) Two friends in a boat search the river with poles. Inscr. (defective): MERSV̄ PIS-CANTVR ME . . . .NTVR ("They fish for the drowned man . . ."). (4) He is laid before a smoking

63

TRINITY CHAPEL XI   TRINITY CHAPEL XII

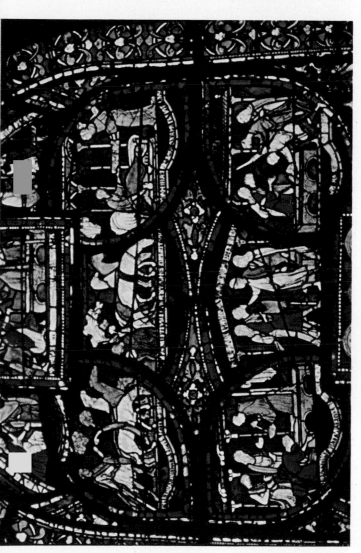

PLATE 6. THE STORY OF RICHARD SUNIEVE. 13TH CENTURY. TRINITY CHAPEL, WINDOW VI. P. 58.

fire in the house of the toll-gate keeper; two women tend him. Inscr.: IGNIB'(*us*) ADMOTV'(*s*) REPARATVR CORPORE TOT'(*us*) ("Being laid by the fire he is restored in his body to wholeness"). There are 15th-century insertions.

5   *Pilgrims.*

6   *A youth kneeling.*

7   *A dying man healed.*

8   *Two men* lowering a green coffin with mauve pall. Inscr.: ..LLV̄ MERENTES THOME VOVERE PARENTES ("The mourning parents dedicated him to St Thomas").

9   *A pilgrimage.* A little boy, lame (perhaps Henry of Beche), led by his mother, his father following. Inscr. defective.

10   *An offering.* A man laying wire on the tomb.

11   Uncertain. A man partly under a yellow coverlet, leaning against a green cloth; a woman and priest stand by. Inscr. mutilated.

12   *An offering* of a coil of wire. Inscr.: FIT THOME GRAT'(*us*) DAT VOTV̂(*m*) LETIFICAT'(*us*). ("He becomes grateful to St Thomas, he is made glad and gives his offering").

13   *A young girl restored to life*, perhaps Cicely, daughter of Jordan of Plumstead, Norfolk. She sits up in bed, two men approach rejoicing, one of them holds out a length of drapery. Inscr.: D(?)ATVRSI CINCS̄C̄S VENIVNT IN GAVDIA PLA(?)NCT'(*us*) ("If the hallowed girdle is given, lamentations turn into rejoicings"). The drapery is perhaps a girdle sanctified by dipping in the healing water.

14, 15 *A boy restored to life*, probably Gilbert, son of William le Brun. (14) Sitting up in bed, he is embraced by his father. Inscr.: ARRID'(*et*) FLENTI PVER ASSVRGIT VENIENTI ("The boy smiles at his tears and rises towards him as he comes"). (15) Accompanied by his parents he lays wire on the tomb. Inscr.: DONA

REDONATO RED[DV]NTVR DEBITA NATO ("Her son having been given back, the due offerings are rendered").

16 *A child's funeral.* A bishop (or priest with high cap) recites prayers whilst a clerk with bucket and brush attends to sprinkle the dead with holy water. Inscr. (defective): DEFVNCTV̄ PLORAT PLEBS P(*ro*) Q'(*u*)O PR[ES]BITER ORAT ("The congregation mourn for the dead for whom the priest prays"). Perhaps part of the story of Nos. 14, 15.

17, 18 *Scenes at the tomb.* (17) Kneelers at the tomb. (18) Pilgrims with a coil of wire. Inscr. (both) fragmentary.

WINDOW XII

The strong blue tonality of the window as a whole is noticeable. The base of each panel is supported on a "bridge". A date about 1220 at the earliest is indicated by the saint's shrine depicted in Nos. 21, 22. Much restoration with modern glass.

1–6 *The child Geoffrey of Winchester.* (1) He lies dying of fever, his mother prays, St Thomas appears, blessing, behind his grandmother. Inscr.: THOME VIRTVTE VIS FEBRIS CEDTT (*sic*) ACVTE ("By the virtue of Thomas the violence of an acute fever is reduced"). (2) Geoffrey makes an offering; his mother helps him to drop a coin in a money-box held by a priest in tall fur cap. Inscr. (defective): ...EM PIETAS FERRO S: NON SINIT ETAS ("... but [*or* if] his age does not allow"). (3) Soon after his recovery, a gale brings down a wall on his cradle, his mother and grandmother are terrified. Inscr.: ECCE REPENTINA PRE-MITVR PVER IPSE RVINA ("Lo, the child himself is crushed by a sudden collapse"). (4) The women and his father among the ruins (largely modern). (6) The mother, invoking St Thomas, swoons, a servant throws water over her, another clears the debris with a pickaxe.

66

Inscr. (defective): ...ANABAT(*ur*) PRIVS T(?)VNC SERVARE ROGATVR (Perhaps "[The saint] is asked to save him who was before being healed [*sanabatur*]—or mangled [*laniabatur*]"). (5) The child is found unhurt among the ruins; among the bystanders, servants with a pickaxe and a felling-axe. Inscr. (defective): MOLES DIRIPIT ...S REPERITVR (Dr Mason restored *ur puer incolumi*, "The wreckage is torn apart, the child is found unhurt").

7, 8 *James, infant son of Roger, Earl of Clare*, cured of hernia. (7) Mostly modern. The child on a bier, the mother demanding a miracle, though the Countess of Warwick and others dissuade her. (8) The child healed with a rag of St Thomas's shirt; he is held up by his mother on a stool by the tomb whilst the water of St Thomas is applied to the seat of the trouble, to which his father is pointing. Inscr.: VENTRI INTESTI(*na*) MONV-MENTVM FIT MEDICINA ("The cure within the belly is testimony [to the saint]").

9, 10 Healing of a lame young man, probably *Eilwin of Berkhamsted*. (9) On crutches, with outstretched arms, he approaches the tomb, on which is a money-box; a woman follows with hands clasped in prayer. His crutches are swathed in cloth against soreness of the armpits and shod with ferrules, as described by the chronicler of Eilwin. Inscr. fragmentary. (10) He stoops to offer a basin of coins at the tomb, the woman holding his crutches. Inscr. (defective, perhaps belonging to No. 9): SVPPLEX IMPLOR[AT] ... *AIGA* PRONVS ADORAT ("He implores as a suppliant ... he stoops in adoration").

11 *A leprous monk* meeting pilgrims. Largely modern (perhaps relating to No. 12).

12 *Tending of a leprous priest*, perhaps Elias of Reading. His arms and legs are spotted with the disease; he holds his left hand to his eyes (mentioned by the chronicler of Elias as watering); a physician points to the condition of his arm whilst another holding up a flask makes a

uroscopic examination, for which compare the relief of Medicine on Giotto's Tower, Florence, and a glass-painting of St Cosmas (or St Damian) at Minster Lovell church, Oxfordshire.

13–18 *William of Gloucester*, a workman buried by a fall of earth whilst he was laying water-pipes on the estate of Roger of Pont l'Évêque, Archbishop of York, at Churchdown. (13) A mound collapses on him as he digs waist-deep in a hole; two companions with spades look back at the accident. (14) The eye-witnesses bring news of it to a priest. Inscrip. defective. (15) Mostly modern. A woman tells that she knows by a vision that William is still alive. Inscr. defective. (16) The bailiff of the estate, who was out riding, his ear to the ground, hears William's groans; another man holds the bailiff's horse. Inscr. (defective):...ACCIDIT & CERT...*SIBI* VM *SVO*. (17) Mostly modern, with fragments of inscription. The priest addressing his parishioners. (18) The bailiff rides once more to the priest's house to tell him. Inscr.: MIRATVR MVL-TVM POPVLVS SPIRARE SEPVLTVM ("The people marvel greatly that the buried man breathes"). (19) The parishioners with mattock and axe go to the spot, directed by the bailiff on his horse. Inscr.: [THO]MAM QVEM DICIT EREPTOREM BENE-DICIT ("Thomas whom he calls his rescuer he blesses").

21 *An offering of wire at the shrine of St Thomas*. Inscr. defective. This and No. 23 are of interest as showing offerings not at the tomb but at the shrine, seen above the altar which was placed at the west end of it; it is supported on columns.

22 *Suppliants at the shrine*. Above, a crown of lamps and a single lamp. Inscr. of uncertain significance: ORABIT SOLA FRATRIS FER ..F *EQVNTV* FRATER.

SOUTH-WEST TRANSEPT
EARLY PANELS IN SOUTH WINDOW

Two panels with figures of the early 13th century, reconstructed with fragments of glass of the same period by S. C. Caldwell, were inserted in this window (compare p. 83) in 1920 to replace panels moved back to their proper positions in the Trinity Chapel. The original situation is unrecorded.

1   *David*, crowned, with harp.
2   *Unidentified figure*, on throne.

WATER TOWER
(Early Glass)
WINDOW I

THIS window retained its original shape when the remaining windows in the Water Tower were reconstructed in the 15th century. About fifty years ago it was filled with a new composition made up by Samuel Caldwell, Senior, out of early 13th-century glass, originally in other parts of the Cathedral, including a medallion with *Christ appearing to St Mary Magdalene* in the Garden of Gethsemane.

WINDOW III (UPPER HALF)

These panels, inserted here in 1900, belong to the same series as Nos. 3, 4 in the East Window of the Crypt (see p. 38)

1   *SS. Bartholomew and Simon*, the latter with spear. Inscr.: S: BA.MAEVS, S: SIMON.
2   *St John the Evangelist and an unidentified Apostle*, perhaps St James the Less, with chalice and club(?) respectively.

These panels are from the same series as those in Window III.

1   *SS. James the Greater and Matthias* (Sᶜ IACOBVS, Sᵉ MATHIAS), with scrolls, one inscribed: CONIV-GATVS (of unexplained significance), the other: ...VS EOR... (*Ivit sonus eorum*, see p. 38).

2   *Two Apostles*, unidentified, one with sword (perhaps St Paul), with scrolls inscribed: CONIVGATVS, IVIT SONVS EORVM, as in No. 1.

EARLY REMNANTS, UNPLACED

St Dunstan, writing in a book. Inscr.: ARCHIEPISC DVN-STANVS. Panel, about 1200; the face, hands, and book, modern restoration based on a MS. in the British Museum. Given by Miss Susan Minet in 1944.

Head of the dead Christ, probably from a *Crucifixion* or a *Descent from the Cross*. Early 13th century.

NAVE

NORTH AISLE

THERE are fragments of late 14th-century glass in several windows in the north aisle of the Nave, of which the rebuilding was begun in 1394. These include the topmost quatrefoil-shaped tracery-lights of the second, third, fourth, and sixth windows from the east; in the lobes of four of them are cinque-foils or five-petalled roses; the fifth window shows Lombardic capitals (NNA) reserved on a black ground, one in each of the three upper lobes, and has original canopy-tops in the main lights.

The first window at the east end of the aisle, by Clayton and Bell, commemorates Arthur Penrhyn Stanley, Dean of Westminster (d. 1881); it includes figures of Archbishops Odo, Stigand, and Lanfranc, and Prior Ernulf, and scenes from the history of the Cathedral.

TREASURY [1]

St Christopher bearing the Child Christ. German Glass. About 1400.

MUSIC ROOM [1]

PANEL, late 14th century. *Three boy musicians*, with lute and harps.

WEST WINDOW

THE glazing of this window is shown, by the fact that it includes at its summit shields with the arms of both queens of Richard II, to have been begun between 1396 and 1399. The original tracery-lights may be dated in this period; the glass of the main lights is of later date, probably about the middle of the 15th century. The two upper ranges of these contained portraits of the kings of England of which the identity is a matter of dispute. The series is recorded as beginning with Canute; its continuation in the lowest range would involve the inclusion of Edward IV (on the assumption that Hardicanute and Harold II were not omitted, on which point there is no evidence); in any case, a date for these lights would be implied not before 1461, which seems impossible on grounds of style. A possibility is that the lowest range was originally occupied by prominent archbishops. The crowns in many cases resemble those of the kings in the "Jesse" window at Winchester College Chapel (about 1400), but the trellis-diapers forming backgrounds to the figures recall those of the windows of the Beauchamp Chapel, Warwick (1447); like these latter, the window was probably the work of the King's Glazier at Westminster. The series of kings originally had their names inscribed in Latin. Remnants of these recorded by the Canter-

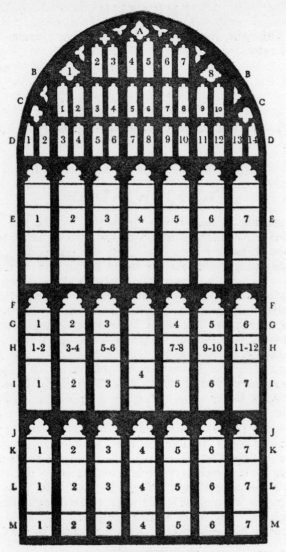

WEST WINDOW

bury historian Gostling in 1779 throw no light on the forward extent of the series; all that now survives is a fragment (unplaced) with the word *Re*[*x*]. Of the kings, only seven in the upper range and one replaced by Dean Bell (1924–9) in the middle range now survive; the remaining lights of the middle and lowest ranges contain figures from the 12th-century "Genealogical" windows (see p. 19), helped out with figure-panels varying in style and datable about the second quarter of the 15th century, from tracery-lights perhaps in the Nave, and heraldic panels, mostly datable after 1450. To fill these out, various fragments, mostly of architectural canopy-work, have been inserted. All the panels which did not originally belong to the window are marked below with an asterisk.

The tracery-lights were filled with figures of Prophets in the two upper rows and with Apostles flanked by angels in the lowest row; figures (marked with an asterisk) from some other (undetermined) part of the Cathedral have been substituted for some of these.

TRACERY LIGHTS

A.   *Arms of Richard II* (Edward the Confessor impaling Quarterly, France Ancient, and England). Richard, out of veneration for St Edward, adopted his traditional shield as an impalement with his own royal coat, as on the back of the Wilton Diptych, in the National Gallery.

B.1   *Arms of Isabella of France*, second wife of Richard II (m. 1396) (France Ancient quartering England, impaling France Modern).

B.2–7   *Prophets*; their identity cannot be distinguished.

B.8   *Arms of Anne of Bohemia*, first wife of Richard II (m. 1381, d. 1394) (France Ancient quartering England, impaling Bohemia). The crown of the Bohemian lions is painted in silver-yellow stain.

C.1–10   In these lights were originally ten Prophets. The Apostles now occupying five of them were (except C.6) perhaps in the West Window of the Chapter House.

C.1   *St Philip, with three loaves (John 6. 5–9).
C.2   *An Apostle (St Simon?), with sword (or scimitar?, with reference to St Simon's martyrdom in Persia).
C.3, 4 Two Prophets (unidentified).
C.5   St James the Greater, with cockle-shell (emblem of pilgrimage to his shrine at Compostella) and pilgrim's staff. This figure was originally in the lowest range.
C.6–8   Three Prophets, unidentified.
C.9   *St Paul, with sword.
C.10   *Apostle, unidentified.
D.1, 14 Two Angels, with censers.
D.2   St Peter, with keys and book.
D.3, 4 Two Apostles, unidentified, one with scroll and palm-branch the other with book and staff.
D.5   St John the Evangelist, with chalice.
D.6   St Matthias, with spear.
D.7   St James the Less, with book and club.
D.8   St Matthew, with scroll inscribed: matheus.
D.9   St Bartholomew, with flaying-knife and book.
D.10   St Simon(?), with banner and book.
D.11, 12 Two Apostles, unidentified, with scroll and book.
D.13   St Matthias(?), with book and axe or halberd.

MAIN LIGHTS

E.1   Canute, with sceptre.
E.2   William the Conqueror, with sword; in niches of the canopy-shafts, a hound and a falcon (or eagle).
E.3   Harold II(?), with sceptre.
E.4   Edward the Confessor(?), with halberd; on the canopy-shafts, hounds and falcons.
E.5   William II(?), with sceptre. On each canopy-shaft, a hound in a niche. (Pl. 7)
E.6   Henry I(?), with sceptre.
E.7   Stephen(?), with sceptre.

F.1–7, J.1–7. The pinnacles of the original canopies remain (perhaps not all in their original positions).

G.1   *Arms of *Thomas of Lancaster, Duke of Clarence* (d. 1421), second son of Henry IV, and *Whittlesey* (for Abp William W., 1368–75).

G.2   *Arms of *Mepham* (for Abp Simon M., 1328–33), and *Langton* (for Abp Stephen L., 1207–29).

G.3   *Arms of *Winchelsea* (for Abp Robert W., 1294–1313), and *Guldeford* (for Sir John G., d. 1493), Comptroller of the Household to Edward IV. Skirts of a figure among the surrounding fragments.

G.4   *Arms of France Modern quartering England*, over all a label of six points ermine (perhaps for John, Duke of Bedford, before 1399), and *Bokyngham* (for John Bokyngham, d. 1397, Bishop of Lincoln).

G.5   *Royal Arms* and arms of *Abp William Courtenay* (1381–96).

G.6   *Arms of *Bradwardine* (for Abp Thomas B., 1349), and *Chichele* (for Abp Henry C., 1414–43). Among the surrounding fragments part of a wing, and legs in hose with pointed toes, from canopy-niches of a lost panel from the series of kings.

H.1,2 *Two *Apostles*, unidentified, one with book.

H.3   *St Peter*, with keys and book.

H.4   *St Paul*, with sword and book.

H.5   *Youthful Saint*, unidentified, with staff, in the act of benediction.

H.6,7 *Two *Apostles*, unidentified, with book and staff respectively.

H.8,11,12 *Three *sainted Archbishops*, unidentified, in Mass vestments, with cross.

H.9,10 *Two *Apostles*, unidentified, one with book.

I.1–3,6–7 *Six figures from the "Genealogical" windows (see p. 19).

I.4   *King of England*, unidentified, with orb and sceptre; in niches of the canopy, small figures (incomplete).

K.1   *Arms of *Folliot*(?) *quartering Warenne*, and a shield made up of fragments; among the surrounding fragments a star, legs (as in G.6 and I.4), and lettering (..*ama*..).

75

K.2　*Royal Arms and a shield composed of fragments, including an object with a lockplate and keyhole; the surround includes part of a fringed vestment, part of the Bourchier shield, an acorn and oak-leaves, and 15th- and 16th-century lettering.

K.3　*Arms of *Thomas of Lancaster* (as above), and *Bourchier* (for Abp Thomas B., 1454–86) : the surround includes legs in hose standing on a pebble pavement, drapery, and toes (on a larger scale), a bunch of grapes, links of a chain, and a 14th-century ivy-leaf.

K.4　*Two shields made up of fragments; legs (as in K.3) in the surround.

K.5　*The *Royal Arms*, and arms of *Arundel* (Fitzalan quartering Warenne, for Abp Thomas A., 1396–1413).

K.6　*Shield charged with the Sacred Monogram (*ihs̄*) in a medallion laid over a processional cross, and the arms of *St Lo* (perhaps for John St Lo, who married Margaret Courtenay) : drapery and part of a large black-letter character in the surround.

K.7　*Arms of *Stratford* (?), patched (perhaps for Abp John S., 1333–49), and *Thomas of Lancaster* (as above).

L.1–7　*Figures from the "Genealogical" windows (see p. 15).

M.1–7　*Panels with shields of the *Royal Arms*, of the latter part of the 14th century. The surrounds include fragments of a 14th-century vine-leaf, a figure on a pebble pavement, an angel's wing, stems with a lily, 16th-century inscription (H. BI), a monster's head and a structure with interlaced spokes.

THE west window of the south aisle of the Nave was filled (1955) by S. C. Caldwell with two figures of kings and shields in canopies; the upper figure has been re-assembled almost entirely (including the head) from ancient glass originally in the middle range of the great West window (see p. 71) ; of the lower, only the face (lower part) and collar are ancient. The shields of Archbishops Arundel and Becket (15th century) came probably from the Chapter House.

WATER TOWER (Late Glass)

ONE window is filled with early glass (see p. 69); the four others were reconstructed, with tracery, by Prior Chillenden (1391–1411). Of these, No. II retains its original glazing in its upper half. In the upper parts of Nos. III and V 13th-century glass has been inserted (see p. 69); the upper part of No. IV has 15th-century glass from other parts of the Cathedral. The 15th- and 16th-century shields among plain quarries in the lower parts of all four windows were placed there by Dean Bell (1924–9), when also the figures in Window IV were brought from the West window, where they had been inserted in place of the king (I.4) now reinstated there (see p. 73).

WATER TOWER
II–V

WINDOW II

1 Arms of *Abp Thomas Arundel* (1397–1414), See of Canterbury impaling Fitzalan quartering Warenne. The dexter half, modern.

2, 3 Two *sainted archbishops*, unidentified, one in processional vestments, the other in Mass vestments.

4 Arms of the *Prince of Wales* (probably for Henry, afterwards King Henry V).

5 *Royal Arms*, France Modern quartering England.

WINDOW III

1 Arms of the *See of Canterbury* impaling a made-up coat.
2, 3 Panels, 13th century (see p. 69).

4   Arms of *Bohun* impaling Fitzalan quartered with Warenne, for Humphrey Bohun, Earl of Hereford (d. 1372), who married Joan, daughter of Richard Fitzalan, Earl of Arundel.

5   Arms of *Cambridge*, probably for Edmund of Langley, Earl of Cambridge (1361–1402) or his son Edward, Duke of York (1373–1415); the torteaux on the label, strictly gules rendered as circles painted in black.

WINDOW IV

1   Arms of *Sir Henry Guldeford*, K.G. (Guldeford quartering Halden) encircled by a Garter inscribed: *Honi soit qui mal y pance* (sic). Shield and Garter about 1530, set in original early 15th-century glass.

2, 3   Two *Sainted Archbishops*, unidentified, vested as in II 2, 3 respectively; between the pinnacles, arms of Beaufort (perhaps for Sir John B., Earl of Somerset, d. 1410) and the Royal Arms (as before 1399), respectively. These panels were perhaps originally in the Nave; they have been enlarged with 14th-century crown borders.

4   Arms of *Abp William Courtenay* (1381–96), Courtenay, with a label charged with three mitres.

5   Shield with badge of the *Prince of Wales*, the "arms for peace" of the Black Prince.

WINDOW V

1   Arms of *Abp Theobald* (1139–60).
2, 3   Panels, 13th century (see p. 70).
4   Arms of *Cambridge* (as in III, 5).
5   Arms of *Beaufort* (as in IV, 2).

CHAPEL OF
ST EDWARD THE CONFESSOR

IN the two windows have been inserted panels from tracery-lights, perhaps in the Nave; they may be dated early in the 15th century.

1   *St Christopher*, carrying the Child Christ.
2   *St Catherine of Alexandria*, with wheel and sword.

SOUTH-WEST TRANSEPT
SOUTH WINDOW

REBUILT in 1792, as originally designed by Abp Chichele (1414–43). What little of the original glass remains is marked below with an asterisk; the inserted panels are partly contemporary with it, probably from tracery-lights in the Nave, partly from the "Genealogical" windows and other early windows (see p. 18). Many of the shields are hung by straps on trees.

A.1, 5, B.1, 10   *Foliage.
A.2   *Arms of the *Priory of Christ Church* (now of the Dean and Chapter).
A.3   *Arms of the *See of Canterbury*.
A.4   *Arms of *Abp Thomas Becket*.
B.2, 4–7, 9   Borders from 13th-century windows.
B.3   *St James the Greater*, with shell on hat and staff; fragments of inscription below (the original title now in B.8).
B.8   "*The Christ of Pity*", displaying his wounds, in a vesica panel, early 14th century; below, 15th-century fragments, including a kneeling figure with chalice, and

SOUTH WINDOW

inscriptions (S. (*Ja*)cobus, from B.3, and *Egfridus*, for Egfrith, King of the Northumbrians).

C.1, 2 *Foliage.

D.1 Miscellaneous fragments, including a head in wimple and crossed hands.

D.2, 3, 5, 6, 9, 10, 12, 13 13th-century fragments.

D.4 *An Archbishop.*

D.7, 8 Angels with censers, 15th century.

D.11 *Half-figure, with crown and book.

D.14 *St John the Evangelist*, with book and scroll with name: IOHANNES AO; 14th century.

E.1, 2, 5, 6, 10, 11, 15, 16 13th-century fragments.

E.3 **St. Margaret*, with barbed cross-staff transfixing the head of a dragon.

E.4 *Monk*, tonsured, with objects of uncertain significance.

E.7 *Female saint*(?), with book.

E.8 *A sainted archbishop* holding his cross and an unidentified object resembling a giant nail (possibly St Denis of France, confused with Dionysius, one of the Seven Sleepers of Ephesus, whose emblem was a nail, or St Dunstan, as a smith).

E.9 *A sainted archbishop*, unidentified.

E.12 *An Apostle*, unidentified.

E.13 *A female saint*, with book.

E.14 *A martyr saint*, with palm-branch.

MAIN LIGHTS

F.K.O. 1–8 *Original pinnacled heads of canopies.

G. Shields of the 15th and early 16th century set among miscellaneous fragments.

G.1 Arms of *Gage*; among the surrounding fragments, "Canterbury Bell" flowers, 14th century, as at St Nicholas, Harbledown.

G.2 Arms of *Wykeham*.

G.3 Arms of *Abp William Warham* (1504–30).

G.4 The *Royal Arms* impaling those of *Bohun*, for Mary Bohun, first wife of Henry IV (m. 1381, d. 1394); the lions of England painted in silver-yellow stain on *white* glass (instead of gules): the surround includes 16th-century fragments with lettering in Roman capitals.

G.5   Arms of *Arundel*; the surround includes a youth's head, part of a seraph, and a horned head with wings.

G.6   Arms of *Abp Thomas Becket.*

G.7   Arms, unidentified.

G.8   Arms, Quarterly, 1 and 4, made up of modern glass, 2 and 3, *Nevill of Raby.*

H.1–8 Figures from the "Genealogical" windows (see p. 18).

I. Panels made up of 15th-century quatrefoils from the tracery-lights of the Nave, with 13th-century foliage. In some of the heraldic panels the shields are hung by their straps on trees.

I.1   *A seraph*, standing on a wheel, between suns; in the surround, a 16th-century console inscribed: [I]VSTITI [A].

I.2   Arms of *Christ Church* (as in A.2); in the surround, part of a quarry with a bird, the hindquarters of a hare or rabbit, part of a book, part of an angel playing a viol.

I.3   Arms of *Criol*, held by an angel; among the surrounding fragments, black-letter inscription and a finial in front of a patterned cloth.

I.4   Arms of *Ufford*; in the surround, drapery and part of an angel's wing.

I.5   Arms of *Chichele.*

I.6   Arms of *Fitzwilliam*, held by an angel; in the surround, a crown, part of a fish, and 16th-century Renaissance fragments including two griffin's heads.

I.7   Arms of *St Augustine's Abbey, Canterbury*; in the surround, 14th-century maple foliage.

I.8   *A seraph* between suns; in the surround, part of an ermine cloak.

L. Panels with shields, mostly 16th century, in some cases hung on trees, among 13th-century fragments.

L.1   *Royal Arms*, late 14th century; in the surround, a man in armour (13th century), fragments of the Bourchier badge and arms of Louvaine.

L.2   Arms of *Beauchamp of Bergavenny* quartering *Clare* quartered with *Despenser*, probably for Richard Beauchamp, Earl of Worcester, Baron Bergavenny; in the surround, part of a face in armour, inscription (*osit*), and 16th-century lettering HO, probably from the Garter motto.

L.3   *Royal Arms*, as in L. 1; in the surround, a bare foot among herbage, and black-letter inscription.

L.4   Arms of *Cockfield*; in the surround, parts of two figures of Christ crucified, and of a griffin.

L.5   Arms of *Parker*(?), incorrectly rendered; in the surround, part of a face (13th century), a tonsured head, an eye, a hand holding a staff or sceptre (15th century), a nose (16th century).

L.7   Arms of *Barnewell*; in the surround, parts of the Bourchier slip-knot badge and falcon crest, and of the Sacred Initials *ihs*.

L.8   The *Royal Arms*.

M.1-3, 6–8   Figures from the "Genealogical" windows (see p. 18).

M.4, 5 Figures of *David* and another (see p. 69).

N. Tracery-lights each containing a shield hung from a tree, (15th century; 13th-century foliage in the spandrels).

N.1   Arms of *John Haute*, of Surrenden Manor.
N.2   Arms of *Hever*.
N.3   Arms of *Abp Warham* (as in G.3).
N.4   Arms of *Holland*; in the surround, fragments of a seraph, black-letter inscription (including *Scūs*, perhaps for *Secundus* from the portraits of kings, see p. 73).

N.5   Arms of *Etchingham*; in the surround, parts of 14th-century maple-leaf quarries and ivy border, and a door with knocker.

N.6   Arms of *Strabolgi*.

N.7 Arms of *Hardres*; in the surround, parts of a hand, toes, and an eagle's legs (perhaps St John the Evangelist), and 14th-century ivy-stem.

N.8 Arms of *Wike*, of Somerset; in the surround, battlements and an oak-leaf.

P.1–8 Shields with the *Royal Arms*, of various periods, hung on a stem or tree, flanked by 13th-century foliage. In the surround of P.7 part of a Tudor rose, of P.8, the head of horse with bit.

Q.1–8 Figures from the "Genealogical" windows (see p. 18).

R. Panels made up of 13th-century glass, with an edging of 15th-century architectural fragments.

WEST WINDOW

MODERN. The *Nativity*, the *Agony in the Garden* and the *Resurrection*. By Christopher Whall, in memory of Ottiwell Charles Waterfield, d. 1898; 15th-century fragments incorporated in the tracery include a hand (of St Philip) holding two loaves, and other parts of figures.

ST. MICHAEL'S CHAPEL
WINDOW I (EAST)

MODERN. *The Buffs (Royal East Kent) Memorial Window*. It incorporates the Regimental Badge and the Arms of Queen Elizabeth I, Frederik IX, King of Denmark, as Colonel-in-Chief, Prince George of Denmark (Consort of Queen Anne), and other colonels of the regiment. By William Wilson. 1952.

PLATE 7. KING. WEST WINDOW.
EARLY 14TH CENTURY.

The original ancient glass of the Chapel has been gathered here; it has been supplemented by copies recently made of the ancient glass. The design of the window consists of medallions painted in black and silver-yellow stain on a ground of quarries similarly painted, with shields of arms interspersed. The medallions are of two periods. The earlier, with badges relative to Lady Margaret Holland whose effigy lies on the tomb in the Chapel between those of her two husbands, date presumably from the time when the Chapel was built (dedicated in 1437); these badges are a *hind couchant*, for her grandmother, the Fair Maid of Kent, and a *greyhound*, with collar and leash, for Thomas of Lancaster, Duke of Clarence. The later medallions, to be dated about 1455, show one of the Bourchier badges, a *falcon* or *eagle* with wounded wing. The quarries forming the groundwork are painted with the twig of oak "leaved and fructed" (i.e., with acorns) of Thomas of Woodstock, Duke of Gloucester.

Of the medallions in the main lights, in four rows (A–D) only the following are ancient: falcons—A.1, A.4, C.2; greyhounds—B.3, C.1, C.4; hinds—D.3.

The shields of the three upper rows are modern; in the lowest row, two are ancient:

E.1   Arms of *Isabel*, wife of Henry Bourchier, Earl of Essex (as on p. 86).
E.2   Arms of *Clarence* (partly restored).

WINDOW III

MODERN. *The Four Archangels*. In memory of Maj.-Gen. Henry Parnell, C.B. (d. 1906). By Clayton and Bell.

LADY CHAPEL

THE chapel was completed about 1455, when Thomas Bourchier was Archbishop. The glass now in its east window was removed about 1672 from one of the north windows. In the top lights of the tracery are golden suns. The remaining tracery-lights are filled with roundels among quarries, painted in black and silvery-yellow; in the roundels are badges of the Bourchier family—a slipknot, and a falcon or eagle with wounded wings. The quarries show the twig of oak of Thomas of Woodstock (see p. 85).

In the main lights are five shields.

1   Arms of *Bourchier* quartered with *Louvaine*, impaling *Cambridge*, for Isabel, grand-daughter of Edmund of Langley, Earl of Cambridge, wife of Henry Bourchier, Earl of Essex, brother of Abp Bourchier.

2, 3   Arms of *Bourchier* quartering *Louvaine*.

4   Arms of *France Modern* quartering *England*, impaling *Fitzwarine* quartering *Hankford*, for Fulke Bourchier, Lord Fitzwarine (d. 1478).

5   Arms of *Buckingham* impaling *Nevill*, perhaps for Humphrey Stafford, Duke of Buckingham, who married Anne, daughter of Ralph, Earl of Westmorland.

One of the north windows has been filled with roundels and quarries showing the same Bourchier badges, partly in old glass.

NORTH-WEST TRANSEPT

WEST WINDOW

THE original window was the gift of John Barnewell (d. 1478 or 1479), of the Salt Fishmongers' Company of London, in memory of Thomas Barnewell, presumed to have been his father (d. 1446); all that remains of the ancient glass consists of three shields in tracery-lights.

1   Arms of the *City of London*.

2   Arms of the *Salt Fishmongers' Company* (three pairs of keys, for Peter, as patron saint, and three dolphins).

3   Arms of *Barnewell* (three beavers).

Remnants survive (the Royal Arms at the summit and two "eyes" with inscriptions) from a window destroyed in 1942, by Ward and Hughes, given in the 19th century by Canon R. Moore. The remainder of the window, by Sir Ninian Comper, was the gift in 1954 of the Freemasons of Kent in memory of *King George VI* and the *Coronation of Queen Elizabeth II*. Above the Barnewell shields, the *Annunciation*. In the upper range of main lights, Queen Elizabeth II and the Duke of Edinburgh with their children, flanked on one side by the Archbishops of Canterbury and York and the Bishops of London and Winchester, on the other by the Lord Chancellor, the Lord Great Chamberlain, the Lord High Chamberlain, and the Earl Marshal; in the lower range, King George VI and his Queen, with the Princesses Elizabeth (Queen Elizabeth II) and Margaret as children.

NORTH ("ROYAL") WINDOW

The window contains glass from designs by two distinct glass-painters and, to judge from the evidence of style, of two distinct periods; as not infrequently happened with large Perpendicular windows of the 15th century, the tracery-lights were probably filled with stained glass before the scaffolding for building the vaults was struck, the main lights being temporarily glazed with plain glass, for which stained glass was substituted later. The main lights were doubtless a gift from Edward IV, perhaps ordered in 1465, when he visited Canterbury, and may be attributed to the King's Glazier at Westminster; the inclusion among its surviving remnants of the arms of Viscount Wells and of a figure of Princess Mary, who died in 1482, seems to indicate that the window was completed in that year. The window appears to have displayed originally in the upper range of lights St George and other saints, including St Thomas of Canterbury (Becket), with the Trinity in the midmost light, beneath angels holding shields; in the middle range, the seven "glorious appearances" of the Virgin Mary; in the lowest, portraits of the King and his family, with angels holding their shields, one at the foot of each light; in the

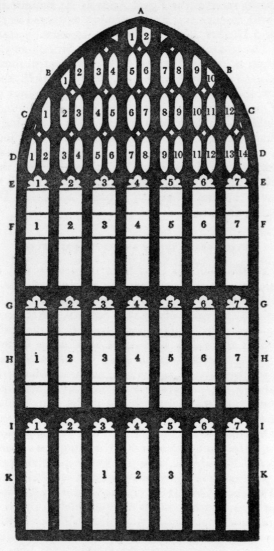

NORTH ("ROYAL") WINDOW

middle light, between the figures, was a crucifix in adoration of which they were kneeling.

Only the royal portraits and the angels holding shields escaped destruction by Richard Culmer, Vicar of Chartham, during the Puritan onslaught in 1643; these remnants were rearranged in their present positions some time before 1774. Various shields were inserted in the heads of the middle and lowest range of lights, and all the main lights were bordered with a variety of painted fragments from the destroyed panels and from other windows; these include scraps of the *rose en soleil* badge of Edward IV, and part of a 15th-century quarry with a primrose.

The tracery lights differ in style from the main lights and are much inferior as works of art; they show the participation of more than one hand either in the drawing of the cartoons or in their transfer by painting to the glass itself; internal evidence suggests that one of these craftsmen was from the Netherlands (see p. 90). The designs from which the cartoons for these lights were drawn are almost certainly the work of a single artist; he was probably a local craftsman, carrying on obsolescent traditions without regard for the new fashions then prevailing, under foreign influences, in the London workshops; his work may be contemporary with that of the designer of the main lights, but was more likely done some years earlier—in any case not before 1468, as shown by the records of the re-building of the transept.

TRACERY LIGHTS

The three rows of lights, below the shields at the apex, contain respectively figures of Prophets who foretold the coming of Christ (with John the Baptist), the Apostles, and sainted ecclesiastics of whom several have some connection with Canterbury.

A.1   The *Royal Arms*.
A.2   Arms of *Abp Thomas Bourchier* (1454–86).
B.1, 10   Half-figures, young men in jewelled hats, each holding a book and a sheet of paper.

B.2   *Isaiah*, with book and scroll inscribed *Isayas*.

B.3   *Daniel*; name inscribed below.

B.4   *Ezra*, holding a crumpled sheet; inscr. below: *esdras*.

B.5   *St John the Baptist*, in mantle over a camel-skin coat, holding his emblem, the Agnus Dei on a book; inscr.: *Iohēs*.

B.6   *Jeremiah*, with book and paper; inscr. (defective): *...emias*.

B.7   *Amos*, with coiled scroll; name inscribed below.

B.8   *Micah*, with book and folded paper; inscr.: *micas*.

B.9   *Ezekiel*, with chain-clasped book and paper; uninscribed.

C.1   *St Thaddeus*, with book; inscr. (modern): *taddeus*.

C.2   *St Bartholomew*, with knife; inscr.: *tholom*.

C.3   *St John the Evangelist*, holding a dragon in a chalice; inscr.: *Iohēs*.

C.4   *St Andrew*, with saltire cross in front of him; inscr.: *andreas*.

C.5   *St James the Greater*, holding a pilgrim's staff with shell attached; inscr.: *Iacob'*.

C.6   *St Peter*, with key; inscr.: *pieter* (the spelling perhaps indicates a Netherlandish painter).

C.7   *St Paul*, with sword and book; inscr.: *paulus*.

C.8   *St Thomas*, with spear; name inscribed below.

C.9   *St Philip*, with cross-staff; inscr.: *philippus*.

C.10   *St Matthew*, with halberd; inscr.: *matheus*. The emblem shows that the painter has confused the Evangelist with St Matthias.

C.11   *St James the Less*, with fuller's club and rolled parchment; inscr. (partly restored with ancient lettering): *iacob' mini*.

C.12   *St Simon*, with saw; head and inscription (*S simon*) modern.

D.1   *St Denis* (to whom Becket commended his cause as he died), decapitated, holding his mitred head and cross. Inscr.: *S dionisius*.

D.2   *St Wilfred* (whose body was sent as a gift from Ripon to Canterbury), with book and cross; inscr.: *S. Wilfridus*.

D.3   *St Augustine of Hippo*, with cross and book; inscr.: *S. augusein* ' [sic].

D.4   *St Martin* (to whom Queen Bertha is said to have dedicated the church in which King Ethelbert was baptized), with cross and book; inscr. (mostly modern): *martin*'.

D.5   *St Jerome*, as Cardinal, with book; inscr.: *S. ieronymus*.

D.6   *St Dunstan*, with cross and book; inscr.: *S. dunstan*'.

D.7   *St Thomas of Canterbury*, with cross and scroll; inscr.: *S thomas*.

D.8   *St Gregory the Great* (the pope who sent St Augustine to Kent), in papal tiara, with book and cross; inscr.: *S gregorius*.

D.9   *St Augustine of Canterbury*, with cross; inscr.: *S. augustinus*.

D.10   *St Anselm*, with cross; inscr.: *S ancelm*'.

D.11   *St Nicholas*, with pastoral staff and book; inscr.: *S nicholaus*.

D.12   *St Blaze*, with cross and book; inscr.: *S blasius*.

D.13   *St Alphege*, the martyred archbishop; inscr.: *S abplegus*.

D.14   *St Audouen* (*Ouen*) *of Rouen* (whose body was brought as a gift to Canterbury), with book and cross; inscr.: *S audoen*'.

MAIN LIGHTS

The panels which were originally in the window, though not all in their present places, are marked with an asterisk.

E.1–7. Angels with shields (only two, E.3, E.6, have their original heads).

E*.1   Arms of *St George*.

E*.2   Arms of Guldeford (incorrectly rendered) quartering *Halden*, probably for Sir Henry Guldeford, K.G.

E*3.   Arms of *Abp Thomas Becket*.

E*.4   Arms of the *Holy Trinity*.

E*.5   Arms of *St Edward the Confessor* (patron of Edward IV).

E*.6   Arms ("canting") of *Lord* (*afterwards Viscount*) *Wells*, who married Princess Cicely.

E*.7   Arms of the *Priory of Christ Church*.

F. Angels with shields of the royal family (only three, F.1–3, have their original faces).

F*.1   Arms of the *Duke of York*.

F*.2   Arms of the *Prince of Wales*.

F*.3   The *Royal Arms*.

F*.4   Arms of *King Ethelred* or *King Arthur*.

F*.5   Arms of *France Modern* quartering *England* impaled with Quarterly of six, 1 *Luxembourg*, 2 *Baux*, 3 The Lusignan kings of *Cyprus*, 4 *Orsini*, 5 *St Paul*, 6 *Woodville*, for Queen Elizabeth Woodville.

F*.6   Arms of *Castile* quartering *Leon*, for Edmund Langley, Duke of York (great-grandfather of Edward IV), who married Isabel of Castile and Leon.

F*.7   Arms of *Mortimer* quartering *De Burgh*.

G.1   Shield with a mitre placed in front of a crozier with a stone below and, on either side, the initials *G* (or *T*) *p^i* (apparently the rebus of Thomas Goldstone I, Prior of Christ Church, 1449–68).

G.2   Arms of *Abp Becket*.

G.3   Arms of *Bourchier* quartering *Louvain*.

G.4   The *Royal Arms*.

G.5   Arms of Christ Church (modern).

G.6   Arms of *Henry Despenser*, Bp of Norwich (1370–1406).

G.7   Arms of *Molleins* (Katherine, daughter of Lord Molleins, married Sir John Howard, first Duke of Norfolk).

H. Royal portraits; the figures kneel at prayer-desks; behind them, curtains patterned half with King Edward's badge (a *rose en soleil*), half with the badges of the respective persons. Of the heads, those of the King and Queen only are original; the figures in H.6, H.7 have been extensively restored.

H*.1   *Richard, Duke of York*. His badge is a falcon rising within a fetterlock partly open. Inscr.: *Ricardus dux Edoraci secundus filius Edwardi quarti*.

H*.2   *Edward, Prince of Wales* (afterwards Edward V). The right half of the curtain divided vertically white and green, with the badge of a single ostrich feather and a

PLATE 8. QUEEN ELIZABETH WOODVILLE.
NORTH WINDOW. ABOUT 1482.

facing p. 92

scroll with the motto *Ic dien.* Inscr.: *Edwardus princeps Wallie primus filius Edwardi quarti.*

H*.3   *King Edward IV.* On the side of his prayer-desk a figure of St George and the Dragon. The curtain with badges particoloured ruby and murrey. Inscr.: *Edwardus dei gracia Rex anglie et francie et dominus hibernie.*

H.4   In the presumed place of the Crucifix destroyed in 1643 are now panels described below (p. 94); the upper panel was inserted some time after 1783.

H*.5   *Elizabeth Woodville*, Queen Consort. Half the curtain patterned with a red flower (pink?) between two buds, badge of Margaret of Anjou assumed by Elizabeth. Inscr.: *Regina Elizabetha consors Edwardi dei gracia Regis.* (Pl. 8)

H*.6   *Princesses Elizabeth* (later Queen of Henry VII), *Cicely* (married to John, Lord Wells), and *Anne* (married Thomas Howard, second Duke of Norfolk). Inscr.: *Dn̄a Elizabeth prima filia Edwardi quarti Dn̄a Cecilia scda filia Edwardi quarti Dn̄a Anna tertia filia Edwardi quarti.*

H*.7   *Princesses Katherine* (m. William Courtenay, Earl of Devonshire), and *Mary* (d. 1482). Inscr.: *Dn̄a Katherina septima filia Edwardi quarti Dn̄a Maria quinta filia Edwardi quarti.*

I.1   Arms of *Abp Becket.*

I.2   Personal arms of *Abp Thomas Arundel* (d. 1413).

I.3   Arms presumably of *Abp John Stafford* (1443-52).

I.4   Arms of *Fitzalan* quartering *Warenne.*

I.5, 7 Arms unidentified.

I.6   Arms perhaps of *Sherley* or *Solers.*

K.1, 3 Angels with shields, probably from Abp Warham's Chantry, built in 1507, pulled down before 1729, with arms of the Archbishop himself and of *Abp Thomas Arundel.*

K.2   Arms of *Scott* of Scot's Hall (16th century).

———————————

H.4(b)   *Royal Arms* as borne by Henry VII and Henry VIII, France Modern quartering England, supported by a dragon and a greyhound, with the motto: *Dieu et Mon Droit*; the panel has a border of white roses. The style indicates a date about 1500.

H.4(a) *St Charles* (Charlemagne) or *St Henry*, with the Imperial crown (his name is wanting), and *St Maurice*, wearing a cloak with border of mock inscription, standing under a double arcade with the arms of St Augustine's Abbey, Canterbury, in the spandrels. The names below the figures (*Sanctus, Mauricius, Sanctus* . . .) have become transposed. The panel is Rhenish, about 1510, probably by a glass-painter of Cologne. It was probably a gift to St Augustine's Abbey and acquired by the Cathedral early in the 18th century. The Emperor is likely to be Charlemagne, who was especially honoured in the Swiss region of Valais, scene of the martyrdom of St Maurice and the Theban Legion; the 18th-century antiquaries Gostling and Battley identified the younger figure as a woman in armour and conjectured the pair to be Henry VI "and his martial Queen Margaret of Anjou" or Edward III and Philippa of Hainault.

WATER TOWER PASSAGE

Two panels in the west window, dating from the first half of the 16th century, were restored to the Cathedral in 1946 by Miss Catherine Athill, to whose grandfather they were given by Dean Farrar; they were originally in the Chapter House, whence they were removed to make room for the Dean's arms.

1   The *Royal Arms*. Early 16th century. Technically interesting for the rendering of the fleurs-de-lis by means of yellow glass leaded into holes ground through the blue glass field.

2   Arms of *Abp Warham* (1503–33) flanked by early Renaissance monsters; above, the inscription: *Auxilium meū a dnō* (Ps. 121. 2). Date about 1520.

In the screen above the door from the Transept, a lozenge of enamel-painted glass with "cutwork" scrolls enclosing the arms of *Archbishop Matthew Parker* (1559–76); below, his name in monogram and the words: MVNDVS TRANSIT ET CONCVPIENCIA [*sic*] EIVS ("The world passeth away and the lust thereof", 1 John 2. 17).

LIBRARY CORRIDOR

(*Enamel-painted glass; for other glass of this type see above*).

1 Arms of *Abp George Abbot* (1611–33). First quarter of 17th century.

2 Arms of *Damaris, wife of Archdeacon William Kingsley*, daughter of Abp Abbott. First quarter of 17th century.

LATE GOTHIC GLASS (UNPLACED)

(*Painted in black and silver-yellow stain*)

1 Roundel with rebus of *Thomas Goldwell*, last Prior of Christ Church (1517–40)—*TG* in monogram and two golden well-heads. Inscr. (deciphered by the late Sir Ellis Minns): *Quē pictura Docet rigidos hic ex pu*[lit] *euros* ("It is he who is meant by the picture that has banished the stiff east winds"). About 1517. Doubtless originally in a window facing east.

2 Quarry with rebus of *Thomas Goldwell*, a well-head flanked by the initials *TG*, with *P*i above.

GREAT CLOISTER

(Modern glass in tracery of arcade)

EAST WALK (opposite door of Chapter House) : *St Gregory the Great and the first four Archbishops of Canterbury*, Augustine, Laurentius, Mellitus, and Justus. By Christopher Webb. About 1934.

WEST WALK: 1. *The Adoration of the Shepherds; A Pelican in her Piety; St Francis* (with broken sword) ; *St Martin.* In memory of Dean Richard Lawrie Sheppard. By Hugh Easton. 1939.

2. *Musicians.* Henry Purcell, John Marbeke, Thomas Tallis, Stephen Langton. By Hugh Easton. About 1934.

CHAPTER HOUSE

EAST WINDOW

English Monarchs and Archbishops of Canterbury from Bertha and Augustine to Victoria and Benson. Given by the Freemasons of Kent. By Messrs Hemming. 1896.

WEST WINDOW

Arms of the United Kingdom and of the Universities and Colleges of Oxford and Cambridge. In memory of Dean Frederick William Farrar (d. 1903). By Messrs Hemming.

SUPPLEMENTARY NOTE

WHILE the book was in the press it was learned that a new window is being inserted at the west end of the North Aisle of the Nave. In the lower half, a sainted king, probably Edward the Confessor (mainly 15th century), in the upper, *St Augustine* (head only ancient).

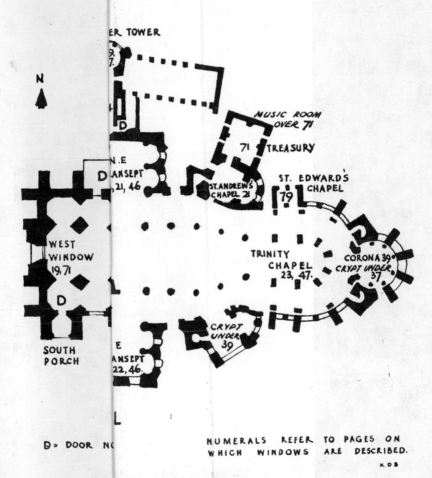

N

ER TOWER
9,
7.

MUSIC ROOM
OVER 71

71 TREASURY

N.E
ANSEPT
, 21, 46

ST. ANDREW'S
CHAPEL 21

ST. EDWARD'S
CHAPEL

79

WEST
WINDOW
19, 71

TRINITY
CHAPEL
23, 47.

CORONA 39
CRYPT UNDER
37

D

CRYPT
UNDER
39

SOUTH
PORCH

E
ANSEPT
22, 46.

L

D = DOOR N   NUMERALS REFER TO PAGES ON
                  WHICH WINDOWS ARE DESCRIBED.

K.D.B

d an advanced stage of production, was
the extra costs involved; the publisher
. Douglas Bundy, A.R.I.B.A., who kindly
plan by the late W. D. Caröe, 1925).